AF251845

PURSUING THE PURSUIT

PURSUING the PURSUIT—
THE BLACK PLIGHT IN WHITE AMERICA

by
Jon Eckels

AN EXPOSITION-UNIVERSITY BOOK

Exposition Press   *Hicksville, New York*

In love and freedom, this book is dedicated to the living, the dead and to the undying—Akhnaton, Shyaam, Nzinga, Shaka, Toussaint L'Ouverture, Dessalines, Christophe, Gabriel, Nat the Prophet, Richard Allen, Denmark Vesey, David Walker, Martin Delaney, Henry Highland Garnet, Frederick Douglass, Harriet Tubman, William M. Trotter, Marcus Garvey, Richard Wright, Paul Robeson, Patrice Lumumba, W. E. B. Du Bois, Ray Duren, Kwame Nkrumah, Elijah Muhammed, Martin L. King, Jr., Malcolm X, Frantz Fanon, George Jackson, Amilcar Cabral, Imari Obadele, and to all of the Great Unknowns who lived and struggled for freedom; and for you who are truly committed to liberation, and are willing to pay the price.

CONTENTS

PREFACE

Though this book in its present form took me some years to write, many of its ideas and insights are much older. Certain essays are from thoughts that went into public speeches, college lectures, newspaper editorials,* television and radio programs and a film† (from the period of 1967 to 1972). Some even date back to my undergraduate years in Indianapolis, Indiana. To be sure, the time and historical occurrences have deepened my knowledge and understanding, but the overall scope of the work plus its implications and importance have hardly changed.

When I started the actual writing, two representatives of New York based publishing companies approached me about my intentions: one even tentatively offered me a contract. However, like Alexander Solzhenitsyn, I withheld my book from publication, but unlike the Russian author, the decision was not wholly mine. Perhaps it might seem strange to some, but the same Western literary establishment that was anxious to publish and promote Solzhenitsyn's protest of an aspect of life in the Soviet Union abruptly withdrew a similar openness to my particular examination of the American (and Western) scene.

I have discovered that it is far easier to write about, or at least have published, exposés of the Watergate scandal, Communism, the Mafia, the sexual lives of celebrities, the Symbionese Liberation Army, dolphin-spying, Adolph Hitler, male chauvinism, etc, than in-depth studies of the logic and designs motivating their particular handling and commercialization. I have found,

---

*"Uhuru," Oakland, California, 1967-69.
†"The Fire This Time," with James Baldwin, Bobby Seale, and Jon Eckels, 1968.

too, that Black writers are expected to adhere to a predetermined role of entertaining "whitey." They have the latitude to entertain by cussing, reassuring or confessing their confusion and the blues, etc., all within the context of white exploitative supremacy and paternalism. In a word, the Black writer is admonished to do what his people are constantly trained to do, i.e., to uncritically react to white actions. A Black writer who not only rejects such presuppositions, but analyzes the reasons behind them and recommends political, humanistic alternatives can usually be described as anomalous, uppity, and unpublished. (We will see.)

The task of harboring and working on the book has not been an easy one. I wish to thank certain of my friends (and onetime friends) who, at one time or another, encouraged me in my endeavor. Chief among them are Nat and Sasha Miller, Gene Williams, Julian Richardson, Gail Cardenas, and Barbara Dugan. Deep appreciation to two of my cousins, Fred N. Cody and Winford Cork; and Renate Krug, Nik Martin, Ndjokolodjo Landa, Alex and Harriet Bagwell, Paola Barbieri, and Tarun Bedi. Many thanks also to Norma Dejournette, Jim Cobb, Giuliana Milanese and Bill Sorro. The untiring support of Carol Brown and William Eckels has been invaluable. I am most grateful for the inspiration of Roy T. Thomas and for the substantial assistance of Elena Eckels

London
August, 1974

INTRODUCTION

Black people in the U.S.A., and in much of the world, are unorganized and politically weak, largely because organized strong factions in Western society systematically prevent the development of autonomous leadership. The Black leadership that is encouraged and allowed to function falls into two categories: (1) those leaders who are made and installed by interests external to and in opposition with the general welfare of the Black population; and (2) other individuals who perhaps were not initially sponsored by outside interests (and who might have even briefly entertained independent ideas), but in time were taken over and controlled by those interests.

Authentic, autonomous Black leaders (or, people who are eminently qualified) do appear, but they fall prey to numerous methods of invalidation. Some are murdered outright, while many others are simply suppressed and censored. They are either efficiently discredited, or not given any "official" credence. Important forums, such as the press, radio, television, the cinema, book publishing, and other significant public vehicles are denied them. Simultaneously, the masses of Black people are conditioned to believe that Black individuals have little or no ability, or right to lead, to speak, to write, and to think unless at least one of the powerful agencies of society grants them clearance and approval. In a word, many Black people are maneuvered into trusting, and paying allegiance to anti-Black institutions, the very instruments of their oppression. (Opportunistic and ignorant petty Black leaders energetically function to maintain the unjust arrangement and the status quo.)

I am painfully aware of a long and criminal history of human exploitation. In my own lifetime, I have witnessed and analyzed the political and economic machinations within the American system and the world view, logic, and values that they spawned. This book, then, is about a reality, the presentation and evaluation of which testify more to memory, perception, and integrity than to artiness and pedantry. It is hoped that the telling and evaluating of this reality, echoing my commitment to liberation and justice, and its integral perspective, will contribute to its change.

Oakland, California
March, 1976

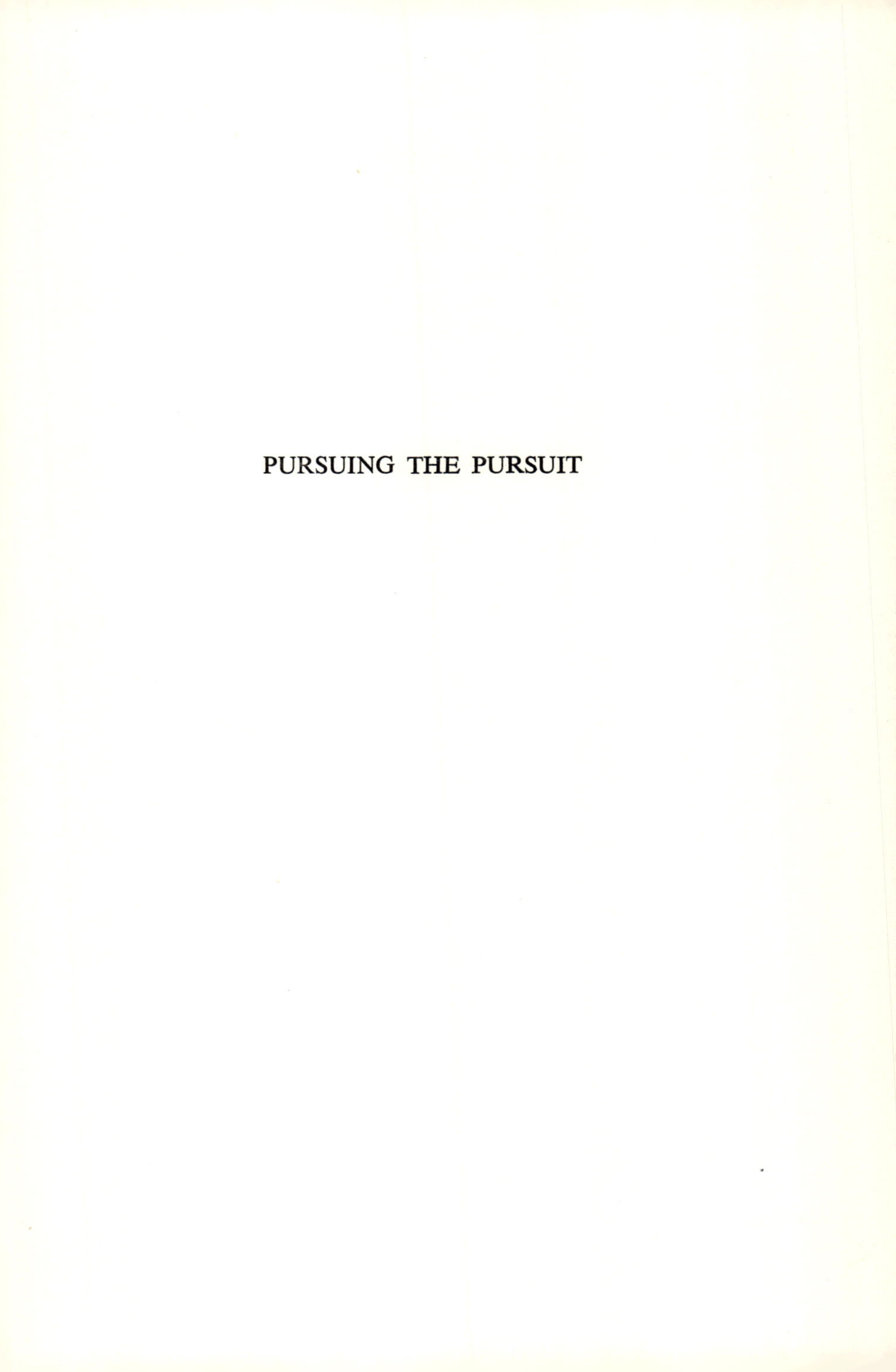

PURSUING THE PURSUIT

We hold these truths to be self-evident, that all Men are created equal, that they are endowed by their Creator with certain unalienable rights, that among these are life, liberty, and the pursuit of happiness. . . .

PURSUING THE PURSUIT—
THE BLACK PLIGHT
IN WHITE AMERICA

The Authorized Version of the history of the United States of America contends that in 1863 Abraham Lincoln freed Black people from slavery. The version is not primarily concerned with what the slaves were freed to. Attempting to save the embattled Union, the President acted on "military necessity" and strategically proclaimed that (some) African bondspeople "henceforward shall be free." Subsequent treatment of African, or Black people, plus the present plights of both Black people and the U.S.A. tend to indicate that Lincoln would have been more successful had he united Black people and freed America. As it was, Lincoln managed to enlarge the "Confederacy" from eleven to thirty-five states and assisted in changing the status of Black people from de jure to de facto slaves.

De facto slavery, or the subordinate condition of the collective Black population from 1863 to the present (excluding the brief interlude of the ill-fated Reconstruction Era), has been a hard, unrelenting reality. The constraints placed on Black people, after the Civil War, while often less crude than antebellum methods, were more ubiquitously binding. Though the period of de jure servitude was often marked by brutality and almost always by unilateral arbitrary actions, there were incidents in the nation where some African descendants were free of the actual bonds of slavery and its demoralizing effects. To be sure, the majority of Africans were held in bondage, but some were free,[1] either at birth, by their owners' actions, or through their own efforts. (Some Africans even owned slaves, Black as well as white. A law in 1680 in Virginia prohibited Blacks from owning whites.) The salient point is that before the Civil War, there did not exist a monolithic, Pavlovian produced African community (or colony) wherein treatment was always uniformly humiliating, brutal, and successful.

Individual slave masters differed in their treatments of and approaches to their chattels. Despite the wretched conditions of most Africans, many actually sought, found and maintained a degree of cultural, social, intellectual, and psychological viability. While some slaves surely must have thought that "the white man's" power had assigned them their low stations for life, people like Benjamin Banneker, Phillis Wheatley, Denmark Vesey, David Walker, Martin Delaney, Jean Baptist Point du Sable and James Beckwourth definitely had other ideas. The new society that was displacing the "Indians" created frontiers for white people, and tolerated a few for certain Blacks as well.

The Civil War, Emancipation Proclamation, and the subsequent end of the Reconstruction Period, more than a decade later, contributed to the reshaping of the society and dealt a heavy blow to African-American" independent thinking, poetry, writing, freedom fighting, "racial" pride, discovery, and courageous individualism. Of course, de jure slavery was never good, nor did most Blacks mourn when it ended; however, unlike the large, city-oriented fledgling capitalistic system, it did not construct unwavering, universal rigid boundaries and restrictions. Agricultural based human slavery was always rather vulnerable to attacks by both its Euro-American and Americanized African detractors, for after all it was immoral, undemocratic, illogical, and eventually, unwieldy. Urbanized capitalism, however, would be another story.

Because of the wealth capitalism guaranteed for the influential few, and the material security it promised to the many (whites), general concerns for morality, democracy, and logic all began to disappear, or they became alchemized by the economic system's highest values. Relative abstractions such as goodness, justice, and reason were left to the disputations of thinkers and the machinations of politicians and lawyers. An amazing transformation occurred—the freed Africans, along with their people in bondage, became "the Negro"—a large, cheap labor device. America's power complex, consisting of people inside and outside of the federal government, garnisheed Black bondspeople from their former Southern masters and lodged them as common property of all of the states. The Negro's status would be that of de facto slave, a national possession to be used for the good of the populace. Almost Marxian in its utility, the commodity, Negro, would serve the interest of all white people, though it/he/she was not to be equally distributed among them. Big business owned (and owns) the Negro.

As long as they considered themselves Africans or African descendants, or a distinct branch of the human family, Black people reasoned that they had a chance for freedom and the pursuance of full human lives. But when they became labeled, abused, and confined as the Negro, a confused state of claustrophobia, demoralization, and panic overtook the people. Earlier, Black individuals had fought for political freedom in America and some even wanted to go (back) to Africa. In 1770, Crispus Attucks was one of the earliest patriots to have his life taken in the cause of America's independence from Britain. In 1815, Paul Cuffe took thirty-eight free Blacks to Sierra Leone. The state of Liberia was partially inhabited by a number of America's exslaves. Even the relatively moderate liberal Frederick Douglass had considered leaving America until the news of the impending Civil War gave him reason for hope (more properly, cause for delusion).

Douglass was not alone in his view; many other Black people felt even stronger than he that the war was an answer to their prayers. Actually, the Civil War, and the Blacks' misreading of it, greatly harmed the Black mentality in America. The people developed a "the good white folks will provide" psychology. The oppressed people were conditioned to unquestionably commit themselves to the authority and good intentions of their great benefactors. Since Douglass' time until now, many Blacks have falsely credited America with waging a Civil War in their interests for the main, if not exclusive purpose, of Black liberation.

Unfortunately, mass deception has led to mass dependency which weakens individual and communal self-reliance. Obviously, some Black people still engage themselves in dreaming a dream that was never meant for them, and pursuing pursuits that only lead to further pursuing. Convinced of the inherent magnanimity of their beloved country, or at least of the liberal white coterie therein, many Black people patiently and expectantly wait for America to give them freedom as a Christmas present, or as a gift during "Black History Week."

During the Reconstruction Period (1867-1877), certain individuals did have a fling at political freedom, but it was all too brief. Their liberty was based on the designs of Northern politicians, the presence of the Union army in the South, and the temporary containment of Southern violence. When Northern politicians changed their strategy, the occupying Union forces were removed and the freedmen were sacrificed to the misplaced, brutal vengeance of the South and the more terrible designs of the nation's business community.

The business community is responsible for placing the Black population in a very subtle, streamlined form of slavery that has proven to be far more unwavering, dehumanizing and ubiquitous than antebellum bondage ever was. To this day, relatively few Black people seem aware of what happened to them and the exact manner in which they are expertly and shamelessly held and used. Many Blacks vent their anger upon and blame poor and Southern "cracker" types for their plight, not realizing that most "rednecks" either moved off the scene at Richmond in 1865, or into the white-collar buffer zone during Franklin Roosevelt's presidency. The remaining visible whites, or the "peckerwoods," are themselves mired in ignorance, indigence, and political weakness; in certain neighborhoods in America, they and the Black poor engage in senseless serial warfare. In the main, however, Black people act in agreement with both the poor whites and the noncreative, insular white middle class on one crucial issue:

they all dance to the tune of and support the destructive system of their entrepreneurial masters. If the people under oppression ever united, there would be a great change in America. First, however, there would have to be a great change in (at least some of) the people.

Because America, at the dawn of the twentieth century, was becoming a strict capitalistic country, definite rules for thought and conduct were constructed and enforced. There would be little space for individual, autonomous Black thought and action and even less for an independent unified community—Black viability would be a threat to the nation. Out of necessity, calculating authority chose leaders for the Negro people who would subscribe to its racist values. It was during the period of the 1890s to the early twentieth century that the image of the ideal "Negro leader," the "yas, suh" boy/man, was forged. Blacks were admonished to accept their alleged racial inferiority, white superiority, and a social position of weakness and political dependency, all for the good of democracy, reason, religion, social practicality, and the economy.

If the Black person wanted to wear the tag "good," he was told to look to white criteria; if he was labeled "bad," it was said that he was acting his "race" or color. After Marcus Garvey's time, Americanized Blacks rarely spoke of going to Africa or being liberated anymore; rather the bolder ones talked about being accepted by or integrating under Caucasians (civil cooperation, not social mixing). Garvey was able to reach, awaken, and organize a large number of people, especially among the poor. He reminded them of their African origins, possibilities and responsibilities, but when his movement failed, many Blacks were thrown into chaos. While some Blacks were discussing, hoping and working for cooperation with whites, their people were being systematically exploited and exterminated, i.e., kept in their "place." A few were exhumed and elevated as examples.

The more the general society abuses and suppresses its Black population, the more the virtue of survival is elevated and praised among Blacks. One often hears Black people discussing the great strength that they have exhibited in surviving amid the pervasive menace of white America. And to be sure, herculean strength was and is required; perhaps a lesser people would have long fallen by the wayside. Owing to the exploitative, greedy, and violence-ridden control that the authorities established over Blacks, and to Black people's own political powerlessness, their very continued existence as a people required tremendous human strength and spiritual depth. Indeed, they had to be a people of faith. Some critics incorrectly evaluate their perspective and life-styles —Black people did not become passive and turn their backs on the earth because they were anxious about dying and strummin' harps "in hebben"; instead, many adopted an orientation to the materialistic society that enabled them to see through and reject its current antihuman myths. Thus, they did not have to view themselves as worthless, inferior animals, fit only for white heels and worldly despair. They were not only human beings, but children of the Most High God.

Out of their vision, many Blacks were able not only to endure amid adverse circumstances, but to love, to oppose injustice, to laugh, to be genuinely compassionate and to retain a vast humaneness that was all but lacking among the more pragmatic, secular majority. From this vision and faith and by the vigor and level of their struggle, the African descendants were able to lend both vitally living music and feeling humanity to North America and to the world. The people of indomitable spirit also were able to keep the hope of freedom and justice alive for all peoples. Being the oppressed who were forced to struggle to survive, Black people had to see the world as it was, and cooperate with it, under their God's direction. Since they were not masters, they had neither the luxury nor the necessity to attempt to falsify and control the earth and its deity. Though now the Black church is generally subverted and much maligned, there was a time when it did save the souls/lives of Black folks. In many ways, the position of survival produced good results, but it had its negative aspects as well.

Finding little redress in the courts and few Caucasian friends who didn't use them for selfish interests, Black people experienced constant frustration. Their small corner in a hostile society became more prescribed and controlled; anxiety, insecurity, and fear became the Negro's normal characteristics. His hatred for his miserable social conditions too often became linked with the feelings he had for himself and his fellow sufferers. Since he was not allowed to show his resentment against his white tormentors, the Negro turned his anger on the Black tormented. Because of his own sense of weakness and his group's general political impotence, the Negro naturally fell into the "system of adversary" that had been made for him and his people. Experiencing both persecution and powerlessness under the monolithic white system, many Black individuals began to blame and penalize themselves or other Black people for their state. Through envy, selfishness, and bitterness resulting from suppressed rage and frustration, some Blacks often victimized their weaker relatives. Through it all, Blacks as a group (and as an economic item) survived.

Survival became an end in itself. One did not survive for self-fulfillment and community. Since the faith had been sabotaged and the vision impaired, one survived to survive to survive. Whereas once the assembly of faith provided some shelter and direction in the raging deathland, disillusionment and psychic disorientation arose. In the absence of adequate space to reach and grow, many individuals spent much of their lives pursuing dull petty concerns, aimless gossiping, and masochistic infighting. In the place of personal faith and community cohesion, a gnawing, usually insatiable need came into being. Opiates in every form substituted for freedom and served as a staple for many Black people. Even music, with its original sacred foundation, often became a commercialized kind of narcotic. An entire multimillion dollar industry (with "soul music" as just one of its products) evolved and guaranteed that Black people would "survive" in the most modern manner. For the past fifty years, being hip has mitigated the pain of being walked on.

Hipness, now generally linked with Blackness, has become an extremely prized asset among many Black people, inside and outside of America. The fatal flaw in being hip, and, conversely, in the contemporary popular notion of being Black, is that the emphasis is placed on stylishly surviving sociopolitical oppression, rather than understanding, rejecting and ending it. Hence, oppressed people who embrace facile hipness and a reacting kind of "Blackness" only succeed in further weakening themselves and placing their lives under the authority of criminal white power. The celebrated now Blackness has been more style than substance, more external manipulated fads than autonomous values and ideas, more wistful delusion than concrete reality.

Black people have not wielded the power to define and develop their community; instead, they have been forced to shape their existence in reaction to alien, hostile forces, and within the context of a highly charged emotional environment, all but bereft of, and in opposition to, the intellectual tools essential for analysis and building. Bare physical survival does not necessarily and automatically lead to intellectual, and spiritual cultivation. While it might be commendable for a smooth slave to survive under his bondage, it is far better for him to risk death in his attempt toward freedom. Rats survive; roaches survive; lice, weasles and monomaniacal bigots survive. A broader concept of survival would assume and assure the survival and elevation, not only of the body, but of the mind, the spirit, of humanity itself.

Modern survival for Blacks means that opiates and diversions are manufactured and foisted on the people as stand-ins for real liberty and power. The more Black people attempt to "survive" using the current tools, the further they get away from psychological and political viability. Likes, dislikes, wants, and needs of Americans generally and Blacks specifically are efficiently produced. Conformity of actions, more properly of reactions, was generally assured. Unwitting Black people are especially victimized by mass conditioning. As early as 1875, Edward Blyden was moved to write about the operation.

> All tendencies to independent individuality were repressed and destroyed. Their ideas and aspirations could be expressed only in conformity with the views and tastes of those who held rule over them. All avenues to intellectual improvement were closed against them, and they were doomed to perpetual ignorance.[2]

In general, the possibilities for Veseys, Delaneys, Walkers, even Wheatleys and Bannekers have long since passed.

Because of their terrifying fear and insecurity, many Blacks can tolerate little individual variety on the parts of other Blacks. Personal uniqueness at worst is a cause for scorn and derision, and at best, a reason for pity. Personal autonomy is viewed as social deviation. The imaginative, artistic child will be crushed by his own peer group unless he has the strength and will to match his sensitivity. Because of powerful divisive opposition, Black people can hardly reach any positive local unity, but they manage a kind of negative national uniformity. In the face of unadorned social brutality, many Blacks wear "the mask" and play it cool. A few others even attempt petty "criminal" acts against whites. Entrepreneurs and racists not only take advantage of Black psychological and political misfortunes, but constantly encourage them. Though many individual Blacks and some groups attempt to help the oppressed, the powerful enemy manages to keep the people off balance politically, and under continuous psychological siege. Some stagger from one faddish diversion to the next, religiously reinforcing the hold that white power has over them.

There have been many genuine attempts to bring justice to or liberate Black people, but thus far they have all failed. Other than the fact that their opposition is powerful and well organized, there are two basic reasons for the continuation of the Black plight. The first is the treacherous strategy that has been used against clear-thinking autonomous victims. Realizing their potential importance and influence among the masses of people, certain segments of authority either refuse forums to positive Black voices or else withhold their credence by suppressing or containing the possible "danger." If, however, an authentic voice (or voices) gets a hearing before Black audiences, the powers that be use all of their wiles to discredit, confuse, and negate the efforts. Occasionally, of course, there have been official directed murders of "uppity niggers," but this strategy isn't as necessary as one might imagine. Economic strangulations, ostracism, or the rare imprisonment of autonomous persons are more subtle strategies than an outright killing. Besides, the smart money does not want to make too many radical Black martyrs, and it knows that petty, envious, and opportunistic Blacks will be only too glad to squelch "one of their 'kind' " who gets out of his place. They are zealous watchdogs of the status quo.

It is these petty, envious, and opportunistic Blacks who comprise the second basic reason why Blacks as a group remain weak. A significant segment of the Black petty bourgeoisie operates as a definite detriment to Black liberation. Its members function as an integral and indispensable part of the machinery of oppression. Historically, because of their close identification with white racial and economic values, they have represented the oppressor's interests among Black people. It was they, under the direction of big business interests, who led the fight to deport Marcus Garvey and thwart his redemption of Africa movement. (By the petty bourgeoisie, I am not referring to those Black people who by their own integrity and ability, despite and without the sponsorship of the system of white supremacy, are proficient and competent at their particular endeavors. Too many undisciplined, frustrated, and indolent Blacks misrepresent and attack strong, emotionally mature Blacks out of envy.) Because the Black petty bourgeoisie generally feel inferior to Caucasians (a natural occurrence since they embrace a racist world view, one aspect of which assigns superiority to whites and inferiority to Blacks), they maintain social distance from them, but they almost always accept, in toto, racist ideology, stratifications, and goals.

Even while advocating "all Black" institutions, the imitative bourgeoisie look to white guidelines and sponsorship. For generations, they have had a stranglehold on the masses of Black people as they have served in their positions of front men for big business concerns. Today, they make occasional shows at advocating Black forms, especially "Blackness" in general (like a new ingredient in an old toothpaste). If they can help to further promote the power of white authority, the weakness of the Black community, and their own selfish interests by wearing bushy "Afro" hair-styles, adopting tinsel-thin "militancy," and even faddish ranting Black racism, they do so. Like their bosses, they have modernized and sophisticated their exploitations of the poor

Black masses. In effect, however, they have changed their techniques and costumes, not their goals.

Since the majority of poor Black people are unorganized, this organized faction articulates and presents its requests to white authority, using as a lever the bodies and miserable plights of the masses. Also, by lauding external glamor, individual "successes," glorious competition, conspicuous consumption, and general capitalistic values, the bourgeoisie confuses the people and further deprecates sharing, discipline, working together, and other positive traits that are essential to freedom and community. In place of liberating knowledge, necessary skills and a new vision of people, the financed, hand-picked, or permitted bourgeois Black leader, politician, preacher, spokesman, writer, etc., in imitation of their sponsors, give the Black folks more diversions, celebrities, entertainment and opiates. This capacity is aptly served by a number of "Black" publications. These organs, like their white controllers, do not value autonomous Black thinking or thinkers; rather, they proclaim and promote apolitical Black athletes, opportunistic entertainers, wily comedians, and slick pimps. The Black youth who can manage to appreciate analysis, critical evaluation, organization, and planned actions is indeed an anomaly.

In 1965, an event occurred that threatened the unholy hegemony that the white entrepreneurs and their Black front men had over the people. Though the rebellion in Watts was unorganized, it represented a very powerful force in America— it reflected the revitalized anger, awakening spirit, and the aspirations of a group of poor, despised people. They were not grinning to get hamburgers, scratching to get jobs, or singing to go to schools. They were not litigating for integration—they were bone tired and soul weary of the phantasmagoria of horror, the obscenity of injustice that was their daily lot, and which an unfeeling crowd either watched dispassionately or avoided altogether.

Watts was important to the Black struggle in America and the world because it spelled an emphatic end to unquestioned accommodation. It provided the psychological foundation on which a Black-controlled, viable political program could have been built. What years of exhibiting public etiquette (i.e., not eating watermelons in public, etc.) smiling on cue, bowing, and legal maneuvering could not do, Watts did: it gave many Black people a new hope, a new strength, a new control, a new feeling about their lives. But before positive, effective action could proceed from it in the community itself, the meaning of Watts was perverted; more policemen, secret agents, fancy clothes and drugs were poured into the area. Business interests co-opted the Watts' phase of the struggle and made its slogans and style marketable items. A few lower class field niggers adapted and joined the ranks of the front men. Predictably, members of the Black bourgeoisie were able to get better jobs and more lucrative positions out of the efforts of that community and the blood of its martyrs.

Just as there had been Watts-type rebellions before 1965, "Watts" did not end in a California ghetto—there would be even more uprisings after that time. Also, organized struggle had preceded Watts and would continue after its fires had subsided. The Black Civil Rights and Liberation Movement reached its apogee in the decade of the sixties and left a powerful, indelible mark on America and the world. Many local and national organizations attempted to awaken and speak to America's "conscience" and change its laws. The Southern Christian Leadership Conference, under the inspiried leadership of Dr. Martin Luther King, Jr., was an example of a national group that worked in the forefront of the struggle for human freedom, justice, and equality. During that time, many activists thought that because the Black populace existed at America's lowest economic and social strata, their Movement's success would act as a positive fulcrum for the liberation of the total society.

If united Black people did not radically rearrange the political and ethical structures of America, they did force it to make certain important (but nonessential) concessions. The Black Movement also challenged the nation's values and raised the political consciousness of its people. Drawing inspiration from the Black struggle, many disadvantaged peoples formed their own organizations and borrowed the strategy, methods, and the rhetoric of the Black Movement. In the United States, many non-Black "minority groups" began to fight for their rights. Not only did non-white minority forces, e.g., Chicano, Native American, and an Asian faction, join in the direct action struggle, but many white ethnic groups also raised their banners. (The militant Jewish Defense League was founded in New York.) In time, homosexuals, lesbians, senior citizens, the youth, and women had their respective movements for liberation.

On the surface, it seemed that at least some of the new groups would combine their efforts with the older, more experienced Black Movement and work to change the conditions and quality of American life. All those who held such hopes were soon disappointed. Opportunism and parochialism within and between individual groups have largely prevented them from effective co-operation. The continuing existence of racism and the strong reaction to it have both been expertly exploited by the power elite to keep the people separated and their several movements ingrown and largely ceremonial. The tool of racism is professionally used in order to insure that the large, poor white working class will remain politically ignorant, impotent, and poor. The divisive tactic of "public school integration" is important to this end. Innumerable Caucasians will patiently endure poverty, economic exploitation, and general ignorance while strongly resisting any threat to the myth of racial superiority (and its concomitant social privileges) based on white skin. Middle-class and upper-middle-class whites are caught up in a self-perpetuating quagmire of personal deception, immorality, and psychosis.

The potential for radical change in America is further weakened by racism within and between the ranks of non-white people. Though the concept of the Third World is valid and important to some individuals in the movements, many more, especially as they are manipulated in their insecure financial circumstances, make few alliances outside of their own "racial" groups. They do not act as if they wish to end America's injustices; rather, their actions indicate that they desire to become a profitable part of them, and at the expense of "less worthy races."

In the 1970s, the Black Liberation Movement has been dismantled almost to the point of extinction. In the main, the influx of the other movements has been used against Black unity and liberation. Nowhere is this tactic more evident than in the elevation and emphasis of a particular segment of the Women's Liberation Movement. The feminist bloc, as it has been exploited and guided by certain external and internal agents, has been used to sabotage the Black Movement, to divide its forces and to obscure its goals. Its divisive thrust has undermined the cause of Black male and Black female unity, while promoting a few myopic, handpicked Black women and rewarding many ambitious middle-class white women, all for the sake of the strengthening and continuation of the status quo. While there is a great need for the elevation of women in the nation's (white) male chauvinistic society, the present Movement has managed to significantly help only a few Caucasian females and hardly any non-white ones.

In addition to being constantly victimized and manipulated by numerous insidious tactics, the Black populace receives the brunt of political repressions and assassinations. Because of the nature and level of the cultural, social, and political aspects of the Black group in America, its people represent the greatest political threat and most viable alternative to the nation's unjust structure. Consequently, violence is no respecter of Black persons, be they Dr. Martin Luther King, Jr., El-Hajj, El-Shabazz, George Jackson, or the many thousands of others discarded in the junk heap of American democracy.

The once extremely lucrative item-negro is being disposed of as waste material—as so much garbage. The nation's penal institutions are crowded with Black bodies. Many individuals seek solace in stylish clothes, aimless partying, alcohol, heavy drugs, reactionary meandering, rabbit-foot religions, and suicide. General confusion covers specific problems.

The barriers blocking general Black awareness, unity, and liberation are many, powerful, and complex. The people are victimized both by the active presence of racism and by expert exploitation of that racism. Few Blacks clearly understand the nature and mechanisms of white supremacy and economic oppression, because their perception is constantly kept off balance by a daily diet of racism and by their disruptive, intense reactions to it. Everywhere they turn, they are assaulted by racist attitudes, institutions, and actions. While their real leaders are discredited, murdered, and silenced, the people are directed to support the very system that is responsible for their continual oppression.

In light of the fact that the descendants of Africans (as the African continent, itself) have been harassed, exploited possessions of the West so long, one crucial question has to be asked (and answered). It is not: Will Black people be free? Rather, because of the wide-scale influence of their white enemies and their Black bourgeois friends, the question is: Do they really want freedom and do they know what it is?

NOTES

1. In 1860, there were about 250,000 free Black people in the South alone. Merle Curti and Lewis Paul Todd, *Rise of the American Nation,* 2nd ed. (New York: Harcourt, Brace & World, Inc., 1966), p. 306.
2. Blyden, Edward W., *Christianity, Islam and the Negro Race,* African Heritage Books (Edinburgh: Edinburgh University Press, 1967), p. 13.

UNICORNS, CHIMERA, AND POWER—ANALYZING THE ANALYZERS

Some years ago, I had the opportunity to worship with and closely observe a few middle-class Caucasian churches in action. I approached the experience with an open mind as I was a student then, and I genuinely wanted to learn. I thought I would witness something very much unlike what I had known in Black churches and in the larger secular society. Time proved me to be only half-right.

Of my experiences that transpired in New England, the Midwest, and on the West Coast, my time spent in a California suburb was by far the most enlightening. The pastor there, like most of his fellow circumlocutionists, was an expert in saying nothing well. He was better than the rest, however, for somehow his sermons were always scintillatingly eloquent and seemingly profound. On one auspicious occasion, the good Reverend announced that "the future is coming." Pausing just long enough to let the idea sink in, he resumed with another gem: "The Pacific is deep and it is wide also." Momentarily, I, even I (with my "crazy nigger" mistrust of fancy phrases) almost joined in the euphoric atmosphere. Yes indeed, I agree, the pastor did preach a good sermon—but what exactly did he say?

A few minutes after I left the church, I concluded the clergyman had said nothing beyond the soothing, self-enforcing words: tvi, jgna cx, sbk, fnk, nzxpt, etc.——or so I thought, until I observed their actual points and tried techniques being further amplified and pushed to more obvious political usages by other, more "secular" experts. Indeed, something was being said and being written; that which was left unexpressed was also significant and a very important part of an overall strategy.

Spinning a seemingly attractive web of piety, certainty, and respectability, the official "experts," be they clergymen, mass-media individuals, literary critics, intellectuals, academicians, or other similar authorities, serve basically the same function; they attempt to flatly deny the reality of the world, at large, or else they try to misrepresent it by interpreting history and events through the logic of their own self-serving sophistries.

The clergymen whom I had heard had little or nothing to do with Christianity, or at least, not with my understanding of Christ's vision—their domain was the middle-class white world view and its regulations that reflected and reinforced the group's place in a capitalistic society. The men of the cloth preached white myths and logic and attacked any thoughts and actions that opposed theirs. Mass-mediaites, literary critics, and academicians are employed in similar functions. With a few notable exceptions, all operate as paid apologists for the continuation of a particular, powerful monolith.

Violence and criminality have been integral parts of Western culture for centuries; without these tools the United States of America would have never been possible. America, the massive tail that now wags the shrinking, moribund European dog, was spawned in bloodshed. An entire people, the so-called "Indians," were nearly extirpated, and the continent of Africa was robbed of its land and millions upon millions of its sons and daughters, all for the sake of the self-proclaimed "superior race."

Though the European continent was itself undergoing vast changes—the diminishing of the authority of the Roman Catholic Church, with the Reformation spelling the end of one age and the beginning of the modern era—the Euro-Americans were subjected to even more radical changes. Not only were many of them already somewhat different from their more stationary and stable European brothers—the colonies were initially peopled by un-desirables, convicts, religious heretics, less than proper ladies, i.e., dregs from the old societies—but amid their new, seemingly unlimited, largely unknown surroundings, the refuse from the Old World began to take on different characteristics more suited to the New.

To be sure, there were European antecedents for American postures, but the small dedicated group so vigorously mixed and pushed the strategies that it had learned that in degree, if not in kind, its policies appeared as a new reality in a new world. The people, too, especially as they came in bloody contact with the Indians and Africans, experienced a significant change in their world view, if not in their psychic structure itself. The relationship that the European invaders established with "red" and "black" people made them "white," successful, and "American." Without the immediate presence of old Europe's traditions, religious authorities and cultures to restrain or direct it, the American experiment, with all its hopes, dreams and excesses, was introduced to the world.

The "new" secularized people, with their mentality alienated from old world order and new world nature and imbued with an odd combination of romanticism and pragmatism, began to pursue their Manifest Destiny. Harnessing the energies and talents of their "melting pot" population, the people went on to world prominence and power. Since the extermination of the Indians and the enslavement of the Africans were usually conducted by a particular detachment of Euro-Americans, some of their fellows could indulge in liberal and idealistic talk, as well as some special related activities. During and after the Revolutionary War (the political fact which ratified the already existing division between the more genteel English colonist and the American subjects), a spirit of celebrated liberalism moved in the land.[1] Perhaps human slavery was wrong—perhaps the displaced Africans had as much right to be free of American control as the Americans had had to be free of British domination . . . perhaps.

Numerous church groups and even some strong individual voices spoke up for democracy and condemned the "evil system of slavery"—especially as it was practiced in the South. From England, John Wesley had castigated American slavery as the worst under the sun. Noble individuals such as George Washington and Thomas Jefferson, either upon their deaths or when they reached old age, actually freed their slaves. Many of these gentlemen, including Patrick "liberty or death" Henry and the sage of Monticello (though he believed in one notion of Black inferiority), gladly demonstrated their largess by sharing their beds with some lowly females. It was widely reported that Jefferson, the respectable author of the Declaration of Independence, sired children by Sally Hemings,[2] his favorite slave-mistress; one can, I think, safely assume that the founding father freed his own children. Undoubtedly, some people sincerely and publicly preached ethics and morality, even if they practiced their opposites.

With the invention of the cotton gin,[3] slavery became more profitable. White moral concern with (Black) human oppression, indeed white morality, outside of the puritan fixation on sex, had to be largely sacrificed. After the Civil War, which witnessed the economic and regional conflicts between North and South, greatly compounded by the presence of slavery, America took a giant step toward her present schizophrenic amoral posture. Native "Americans" were portrayed as savage for defending their land; Africans who fought for their freedom were labeled violent. Materialism left little room for spirituality, or even common sense. Industrialization became more important to the North and the South—sophisticated capitalism grew and became entrenched as number one on the democracy's priorities. The *Nation,* an influential Northern periodical, flatly stated: ". . . the Negro will disappear from the field of national politics. Henceforth, the nation will have nothing more to do with him." Of course, "the Negro" did not disappear; his position and his fate only became, thenceforth, more controlled and predictable.

Where once many people, especially in the North, thought the delineation between right and wrong, good and evil, just and unjust were clearly drawn, now they weren't so sure. When Black servitude became instituted within the structure of the "Republic," and those who were classified as white stood to gain by Black exploitation, Caucasian moral leadership began to metamorphize into respectable gray moralism. Where once the (publicly designated) "madmen," Thaddeus Stevens, Charles Sumners and John Brown, thundered for freedom and social justice, a new, expedient society emerged, which in time witnessed Norman Vincent Peale, Billy Graham, and a host of lesser brethren counseling law 'n' order, rabbit footism, and be-kind-to-your-fine-feathered-friends if-you-can edicts.

The star-spangled "new morality" could not stem the old inhuman immorality nor, for that matter, was it meant to; the new morality modernized thievery, acquisition, and slaughter, while holding guilt to a minimum. Neo-Europe, of course, did not invent greed, lying, and killing; its architects only perfected and nationalized them. What was once viewed as sin, crime, or expressions of social aberrations became required tools of the fledgling young "culture." Those who chose not to come to grips with the major fact of their nation's existence would not see (or fully recognize) the crimes done against "minorities," for their sakes and in their names.

The horror that the Africans experienced was an integral and essential element of the wealth and material well-being of Western Europe and America. For a time, all white people would be confronted with the choices of admitting their complicity in a criminal, antihuman system or else submitting to a radical over-hauling of their moral and intellectual apparatus. (In order for the society to work efficiently, its many contradictions had to be "swallowed whole.") The moral degeneration and spiritual deadness of modern Western societies indicate clearly how most choose.

A world view evolved that, in part, depicted Africans in three categories: grinning, shuffling "good niggers"; the uncouth, bad "uppity niggers"; and the "coloreds." The privileged felt safe since their ears were attuned to hear only what they wanted to believe—good niggers sing, bad ones cuss, and the coloreds say nothing. The poor whites, as well as Blacks, were proper grist for the mill. Only a spiritual and intellectual airtight, antihuman system could label and treat sacred human beings as subhuman beasts. Yet, the system spawned many staunch promoters. They baptized themselves true believers of democracy, free enterprise, and civilization while labeling their victims, who had the audacity to defend themselves, militants, uncivilized, radicals, terrorists, extremists, or at least, uppity. Both Black and white people were (and are) affected by structured white supremacy that sent its contagion throughout the earth. Third World people everywhere are placed on the defensive and depicted as aberrant demi-humans by criminals who palm themselves off as the good, the true, and the authorized.

The rising economic system promised something for every-body, for a price. In time, (almost) everybody was going to be able to pick themselves up by Black people's bootstraps and become equal (robots). Black people, or "the Negro" as they became known, were to be the capital in capitalism, the sine qua non of the young nation's life. Two things had to occur in order for this system to take root and remain secure—both the whites and the Negroes would have to cooperate.

In time, many whites would be infected, and all would receive some secondary advantages from the system; through this method, along with the training that they picked up from related advertise-ment, the general white mentality was shaped. The Blacks would, of course, be another story. Two factors were utilized in order to guarantee the control of Black exploitation and thinking. Most segration laws that America used against Blacks were manu-factured after the Reconstruction Era, immediately preceding the dawn of the twentieth century. The Supreme Court, in 1896, in its infamous case of *Plessy* v. *Ferguson,* upheld the doctrine of "separate but equal," and thereby greatly assisted in establishing the policy that white America was going to adopt in respect to the Negro. "Separate but equal" was the polite code for white supremacy. This dignified thrust gained credence, support, and believers throughout the spheres of the white world. The general clergy, educators, media hustlers, and intellectuals were greatly infected by and became carriers of its ideas. If Black people themselves did not accept the message and attendant values of white supremacy and Black inferiority, there would be other, more brutal ways to convince them of this very practical "truth." White bigots, conservatives, and liberals all contributed to Black people's general miseducation.

In the wake of inchoate liberalism's demise, petty, pious hypocrites arose: in the eyes of many Black people, the "white liberal" became an appellation of scorn. Crude religionists and pseudoscientific academicians incorporated anti-Black sentiments and pronouncements in their dictums, while the more sophisticated experts conveniently ignored the presence and plight of Black people. A religion without morality emerged.[4]—intellectualism without intelligence proliferated. Such American experts, of course, had antecedents in antiquity and in the European medieval period—both platonic dualism and the general metaphysics of the Dark Ages militated against worldly realities—but they also had their own homegrown example to embrace. Ralph Waldo Emerson (1803-1882) and his philosophy of transcendentalism served as a direct link to Yankee solipsism. Singing of, for, and by America, Emerson articulated a system that made it possible for lofty-minded individuals to repose their heads in the comfortable sands of Arcadia while the rest of their bodies graced the "uncouth, other, lower world." In a very famous, and alleged sublime statement, Emerson laid the intellectual foundation for what would later be twisted by smaller, more opportunistic minds into a rationale for ignoring social crimes while receiving their benefits. This American scholar said: "There is nothing, at last, sacred but the integrity of your own mind." As understood and applied by an honest person such as Henry David Thoreau, the idea can lead to a courageous indivduality that reverses its own dignity and the dignity of others. But when the meaning is used by crass, less humane minds, it can supply the impetus and rationale for myopic and selfish individualism. Communication agencies, universities, religious institutions, and other assorted ivory towers house prime examples of this perversion.

The experts are never more active or "clever" as when they are defending sharp and potent challenges to their master's system and their own "removed" but comfortable place in it. Especially when they pass themselves off as literary critics, they presume to set the criteria for all literature, that of the past as well as present-day writings. They prescribe what is great and classical from yesterday, drawing almost exclusively on bourgeois British writing. They, too, insist upon singing, cussing, and silence from Black authors. Hence, autonomous, authentic writings by Blacks rarely if ever come before the public's attention.

Some of the avant garde writers and thinkers actually admit that there are real problems in our midst, but they are confident that they have the answers—exploit sex and violence; abortions; vasectomies; expand and add to mechanics in sex; (middle-class white) women's liberation; "counter" culture; exalt (white middle-class) youth under thirty (for their virtue: they are under thirty): read and promote protest literature against Russia written by Russians, especially of the stripe of the celebrated, simplistic Solzhenitsyn;[5] and since the Beatles are gone, revere the Rolling Stones. Also, one should elevate John Wayne and romanticize some (departed) American Indians; embrace the 30s, 40s and 50s; animate a fairy-tale Jesus, or spruced-up reel-life dirty birds; and allow a Black man to win in an exploitative, white-controlled movie. Or as lost men themselves, the more sophisticated recommend world-hatred and hell for everybody.

In the main, American white writers and intellectuals are in a constant flight away from their sordid history, their psychotic predatory culture, and the true stories of Blacks, the Indian, the Chicano, and the European—which is to say, themselves. Instead of wasting everybody's time in lambasting the state of Black writing, white writers might do well to construct some honest literature of their own. Two whites who tried were the artist who created the comic character, "Krazy Kat," and the meditative Emily Dickinson. Recently, it was admitted that the person who created Krazy was a (light-skinned?) Black man, and it is common knowledge that Emily had the good sense—since she knew that she could not change the nation—to remain single and lock herself in her room for most of her natural life.[6] Another author who deserves honorable mention is Samuel L. Clemens. He did the best he could with what he had, but the America he wanted to recapture never existed. It was as fanciful as Huckleberry Finn, Tom Sawyer, and Mark Twain.

The experts, whether they don the garbs of literary men, or whatever clothes fit the occasion, in addition to attacking the uppity Blacks, continually deal with form and not content. The reasons are, I think, obvious—if they ever seriously paid attention and even partially gave credence to what non-white, authentic voices were saying, they would likely have to give up their claims and credentials as experts. (One aspect of general Black oppression is the 50,000,000 Africans who were slaughtered on their way to the glories of Western civilization—their survivors went on to become bigger and better things.)

Vaunted American institutions, such as the religious syndicates, universities of the stripe of Harvard, Yale and "Ole Miss," the Pentagon, FBI, CIA, CBS, the Rockefellers, Fords, Mellons, Time Magazine, Phi Beta Kappas, and the Daughters of the American Revolution, might, at least, exercise a little more general humility and occasionally pause to give thanks to their Indian and Black benefactors for making their great prestige, power, and wealth all possible. They might have to make their own ways in this world without the protective mechanism of white supremacy that is always operated at the expense of non-white human beings. Black voices, of course, are not perfect; they should and must be evaluated, but by people who listen and think, not by programmed schemers who are full-time defenders of the status quo and hustling hucksters of structured nonsense.

As contradictory and irrational as such white expertise is, it is nevertheless based on internationally promoted white authority, which itself is predicated on the very real presence of devastating firepower. This is the authority that decides who shall live and who shall die. Though the experts and authorities cannot honestly answer or refute the Patrice Lumumbas, the Che Guevaras and the Martin Luther Kings, they can murder them and then attempt to explain them away.

It is then small wonder that the sinister experts can and do examine, analyze, define, and explain everything in the universe except the real basis for their expertise and authority. One could

call their continuing arrogance in the face of their great unwilling-
ness or inability to come to grips with the real world, evil, or
madness, but the theological foundation for evil has been out-
lawed and banished while madness has been transformed into
a modern virtue. Yesterday's sins, selfishness and inhumanity, are
today's ethical norms and political necessities. Thus, the average
American is neither good nor bad. The classical American character itself is little more than a set of romanticized reactions to
capricious predatory power.

Were it not for entertainment, professional sports, drugs,
alcohol, and other assorted "circuses," the nation's analysts and
morticians would be billionaires. The people who are painted as
the aberrant and unsavory characters are often those who reject
standards and values of this society and seek to help to make
the world liveable for human beings. They are called irresponsible,
criminal, radical—in essence, the unauthorized individuals. The
United States of America, as well as much of the West, busies
itself with fighting the bugaboo "Communist menace" (while expediently exploiting it), and especially the insidious dangers
of Adolf Hitler and his Nazi forces. Movies, television shows,
and books are still being produced that warn the world of Hitler's
devilish nature and designs, in spite of the fact that the little
dictator has been dead for over a quarter of a century and his
erstwhile German followers are either dead or else firmly entrenched in the camp of Western "democracies." By turning the
spotlight on Hitler and the past, the present-day tyrants think
they can escape detection and continue unmolested on their way
to total world conquest and control.

Much mileage can be gotten out of the Hitlerian ruse. The
Western powers, which deserted the Jews and often assisted
Hitler in destroying them, can now assuage their public guilt,
ostentatiously exploit their expedient friendship with world
Jewry and, at the same time, cover up their imperialistic designs
and deeds, especially in Africa, the Mid East, Asia and Latin
America. Their audiences are constantly told, "Hitler killed six
million Jews," but few public voices tell us either the amount of
people that racist imperialistic nations killed in the past, or how

many they are murdering today. It appears that the American Indians, the Latinos, Blacks in South Africa, Rhodesia, and America, the Vietnamese and other "minorities" who do not have powerful lobbyists in Washington D.C., or wealthy contributions to the national Republican party, are not very important.

The basic difference between Hitler and today's antihuman dictators is two-fold—style and timing. Hitler was honest about his beliefs and goals; he believed in Aryan supremacy and wanted to control the world, he started an outright attempt to slaughter people of "inferior races." The modern Hitlers are much more hypocritical and sophisticated in their approaches than was the Führer in his; they also utilize white supremacy but instead of preaching and practicing, they only practice. While pontificating on "equality," "nonviolence" and peace, they routinely and ruthlessly pursue their policies of neoimperialism. They do not have to blatantly murder "inferior races" (though they often do), but by tossing out their assimilationist nets—lined with traitors' pittance and gaudy Western values—the poor unfortunates are induced to kill themselves. While Hitler used guns, the gas chambers, and the SS, today's urbane oppressors use massive brainwashing-propaganda tools, demoralizing and divisive tactics, and the nihilistic drug culture.

Hitler was wrong, they say, and from their standpoint, indeed he was. He made two glaring errors: (1) though the Nazi leader shared many of the values and goals of other Westerners, by applying and pursuing them with such naked, brutal force, he exposed the game plans of his cowhite supremacists and threatened to monopolize the game; and (2) lost the war.

In an ironic turn of events of history, many of the major Western powers have joined together in order to depict and demean General Amin of Uganda as "another Hitler." Since the man announced his intentions of helping the people of his country and protecting them from foreign exploitation, the Western presses have vilified and slandered him. Perhaps it is coincidence, but as Amin attempted to rectify some of his country's problems, which were caused by British imperialistic policies, he was called a "racist." Unfortunately, most people outside of Uganda are permitted to see Amin only through the programmed eyes of the West's zealous apologists and its journalistic mercenaries. By highlighting and ridiculing their version of an "African tyrant," they attempt to further discredit Black leadership and deny the right of Black people to govern themselves. Simultaneously, white authority is justified, elevated, and promoted. According to the transparent line, Britain and the Western European nations are good, and South Africa and Rhodesia are not too bad. The U.S.A., of course, is great. (Above all, they are legitimate.)

Yes, the victims are told, the great social crimes are all in the past. And even if America was slightly guilty of such political trespasses, it was the Americans of generations ago, and surely not today's enlightened citizenry. "We must proceed with calm and objective reason; all that is needed now is to educate the disadvantaged and enable them to prepare themselves for 'full citizenship.' They must, above all, obtain their own dignity and identity on their own." The truth, of course, is that the early Americans did not only enslave, kill, and exploit their minorities, but they constructed a political and philosophical apparatus that continues to enslave, kill, and exploit its victims even to this time. Present-day whites are not implicated in the general and specific crimes of their culture because of the hue of their skins or what their ancestors did, but because of what they themselves are doing, and the larcenous structures and values that they are maintaining.

The machinery of injustice does not run on its own volition, nor is it operated by the president alone (be he a Johnson, a Nixon or a Porky Pig), though the high government officials, backed up by the police—domestic and foreign—play a major part in the nation's direction and practices. The business of America is still business—big business—and it is these corporate cliques that control the country. Through the manipulation of human greed and need, many individuals are transformed into petty "criminals." Even presidents and lesser politicians are witting henchmen for the true owners. Congress as the true representative of the people is increasingly becoming a sick joke. The higher the office the politician holds, the more apt he is to take his orders from wealthy, well-organized special interest groups. Indeed, before he is elected, he makes specific commitments to various power blocs, while giving his constituency refurbished generalizations and empty platitudes. Every two or four years, he will likely follow the public rituals of kissing babies, wearing Indian regalia, smiling with Mexican-Americans (in Los Angeles and Texas), shaking hands with Black Baptist ministers, and eating a wide assortment of ethnic foods; but his heart, soul, and influence go with the big money. The majority of the mystified people, who put him into office, are ultimately disappointed as their elected leader works against their collective welfare.

The best hope for the American people, at present, would be to elect individuals who come from the populist tradition, and who are committed to its humanitarian and democratic principles.[7] For all practical purposes, the American society does not now concern itself with the well-being of the "little man" and "little woman." Non-populist politicians, be they liberal, moderate, or conservative, jump to the tune of highly organized, wealthy interest groups. It is these groups that have power over the masses of people, and it is their collective will that takes precedence over the people's general welfare. If it were given a chance, populism could very well help to change the structure of present-day America and contribute toward the liberation of all of its poor exploited people, white as well as Black, and others.

The main force that has worked against populism, of course, has been the special interests groups. In addition to spending millions of dollars to promote hand-picked politicians who will serve their national and international interest, they also finance campaigns against populist-oriented candidates. Another factor that has not helped the cause of populism has been the character of certain populists themselves. Instead of tapping the hidden resources of the people's potentials for unity and social justice, some individuals have unwisely sown widescale polarization and political impotency. By seizing upon the already abused Black population as a convenient scapegoat, they have exploited the prejudices of poor whites and inadvertently helped to maintain the oppression of both people.

The American Declaration of Independence states that the people have the definite right to rid themselves of an unjust rule;[8] the current criminal authority strongly disagrees.

Contemporary successful politicians need not be gifted, nor even intelligent men, only expedient, given to lying, ambitious, and enamored of the status quo. Makeup men, Madison Avenue, and many people's fears, and gullibility do the rest. The yeoman's job actually falls to the punctilious expert; it is these apologists (whether they function in churches, universities, or the mass media) who actually convince the people of the rightness of wrong, that down is up, the reasonableness of madness and the desirability of death as the way of life.

Now it is rather difficult to know which will come first for the American experiment, the twenty-first century or national destruction. While many Americans boast to the world that their country is the biggest, strongest, richest, and best in the universe, it gives every indication that it is suffering from a congenital terminal sickness. Even while bragging of its stability, through the assistance of its highly advanced technology, America is rapidly running away from itself. For the nation does not, as it presently maintains, have a problem—its construction and operation make it The Problem.

Just as there are three colors in the American flag, the nation itself has three main divisions. The first contains the lofty words and ideals of the Constitution, the Declaration of Independence, Lincoln's Gettysburg Address, the Statue of Liberty, etc. It is blue; the America on paper. The second (or red America) is the arena of the struggling people. The concrete reality of oppression and injustice on this level is often avoided, and usually mitigated by manufactured fantasy, illusion, scapegoats, and other forms of constant entertainment. The third division is the power one—the big business clique that owns and directs present-day America, its politicians, and its people. Individuals within this white section cynically pursue their own interests despite the collective welfare of the nation and the world. Their lust for power, avarice and amorality (characteristics that they share with their coautocrats of the earth), not the resistance to them, are the prime causes of worldwide violence. If America's people learned the tripartite nature of their state, they would take a great step toward their liberation.

Occasionally, despite certain self-serving national myths that they were sworn to uphold, some American presidents attempted to talk sense to the American people. Thomas Jefferson admitted that he shuddered at the future fate of slave-holding America when he considered the existence of a just God. Abraham Lincoln avowed that if the country were to be destroyed, it would be from within. Dwight Eisenhower warned against the "military-industrial complex." John F. Kennedy told his nation, "When peaceful change is made impossible, violent change becomes necessary." After Lyndon Johnson left the White House, he attempted to convince America that the welfare of its oppressed Black population was vital to its own. A former vice-president, the now discredited Spiro Agnew, recently talked about the "disastrous" U.S. Middle East policy. He placed the blame on a powerful special interest group—the "Zionist lobby." The current state of nation and world affairs indicate that sensible counsel has largely fallen on deaf ears. Two inexorable laws remain, however, that even imperial America can neither ignore, abrogate, nor abridge:

1. An unadmitted and unfaced dilemma is an unsolved one
2. Sow the political wind, reap the social whirlwind

Or, to paraphrase Hazrat Ali: to fix even a single unlawfully acquired stone in a house guarantees its destruction.

NOTES

1. In 1773, Patrick Henry said slavery was "as repugnant to humanity as it is inconsistent with the Bible and destructive to liberty." Massachusetts' Superior Court ruled that every slave within the state had been freed by the Constitution of 1780.

2. Lerone Bennett, Jr., *Before the Mayflower* (Baltimore, Maryland: Penguin Books, 1966) pp. 258-59.

3. Before the invention of the cotton gin by Eli Whitney in 1793, Thomas Jefferson and many others thought that slavery would disappear in the United States. It did not. The number of slaves in the South increased from about 1,000,000 in 1800 to 4,000,000 in 1860.

4. The "religion" that first transgressed, then transformed and translated Roman Catholicism, Judaism, and Protestantism was a slick blend of moralism, patriotism, and materialism; it was and is called Americanism."

5. In 1974, both Henry Kissinger and George Meany publicly invited Alexander Solzhenitsyn to make his home in America. He graciously refused at that time.

6. The poet who never had a book published in her lifetime once wrote:
   > Assent and you are sane;
   > Demur, you're straightway dangerous
   > And handled with a chain

7. In their platform of July 4, 1892, the populists announced:
   > We meet in the midst of a nation brought to the verge of moral, political and material ruin. The people are demoralized. . . . The newspapers are largely subsidized or muzzled; public opinion silenced; business prostrated; our homes covered with mortgages; labor impoverished; and the land concentrating in the hands of the capitalists. . . . We have witnessed for more than a quarter of a century the struggles of the two great political parties for power and plunder, while grievous wrongs have been inflicted upon the suffering people.

8. ". . . that whenever any form of government becomes destructive of these ends [life, liberty, and the pursuit of happiness], it is the right of the people to alter or to abolish it, and to institute new government. . . ."

FIELD NIGGERISM AND BLACK MILITANCY— A DECADE OF BLACK MILITANCY: 1964-1974

Nobody Knows My Name (1961) is a title of one of James Baldwin's earlier books. Speaking as a Black man, and undoubtedly for numerous Black people, Baldwin clearly announces to the world that he is not a "boy," "Negro," or a "nigger." What he and they are must be a matter of self-definition. As important as the proclamation was for the Black psyche and the Black Movement itself, many subsequent political events in the United States of America served to sabotage and truncate bold expressions of Black independence.[1]

If the above statement bespoke of psychological freedom for some, it also indicated great confusion for others. When one was a boy, a Negro, and/or a nigger, one knew who one was—one had an identity and the security of a "place." But in the absence of a known quantity, one is left without any substance at all. For sanity's sake, "invisible men" have to be visible, at least, to themselves. The question arose: "Then, who are you?" "Black" became the acceptable and timely answer, but its broad amorphous base did not always lend itself to the more particular, honorific interpretation that many activistic militants sought for themselves. Thus, for some, the proud answer was—"I'm a 'field nigger,' myself!" Among this group, a certain segment even exulted at being the "wretched of the earth." A cultural process evolved that featured the elevation and romanticization of the lowest common denominator of the Black community. Ingredients of adventurism, antirationality, and racist, white-induced Black pathology went into the making and marketing of the new "now" nigger.

The two groups called "house niggers" and "field niggers" appeared as an American cultural phenomenon during the nation's period of de jure slavery.[2] The social stratification of the slaves resulted from their functions on the plantation; the house niggers, or "colored people" (as some liked to be called), were those who had the comparatively lighter housework, amid genteel surroundings, while the field variety labored hard, out in the open, with little or no opportunities for "cultural refinement." By their proximity to the master, the house niggers more readily acceded to many of the beliefs and customs of the whites—in fact, some of them actually began to view and accept the master's causes as their own. By osmosis, as it were, many of the house servants began to exemplify the ways of white folk, and by a process other than simple diffusion, some of them actually began to take on the physical features of the Caucasians.

Field niggers, who in the main were not treated as domesticated pets, were generally illiterate and ignorant of the "finer points" of life that white "enlightened and aesthetic" training could have given them. All they had as their daily guides were the lessons that they had learned from the rigors of brutal slavery and the ones that they had retained, valued, and nurtured from Africa. Though there were incidents of communication, affection, and even brotherly cooperation between house and field slaves, a general cleavage did arise that was actively aided and abetted by the slave masters. Being dissuaded from reveling in the remnants of their African past, the house servants constructed a way of life of their own, which largely consisted of collecting crumbs and embracing white values. Out of the reality of unadorned slavery and the residue of African culture, the field slaves created the sublime "Negro" spirituals, the forerunner of all Black music, and the general Black life-style (and laid the foundation for much of the present, Western white "counter" or "youth culture").

For many years in America, up to and even beyond the

period of paper emancipation, the Blacks who received any societal privileges and praises beyond their fellows were the house, or house-type niggers. (This practice still remains in official American circles.) The end of de jure slavery witnessed the exodus of most of the slaves from the immediate area of the plantations, but many of them took their plantation mentalities with them. In order to achieve public recognition and white-supported "success," a Black person had to accommodate white supremacy and emulate as many minor features of white posture that were permitted to him. Thus, the formula for Black "success," and in most cases, Black survival, was—do not challenge or question white supremacy; express no hostility (against whites), or for that matter, do not show too many other complicated human emotions; accommodate, accommodate! Of course, not all Black people accepted the formula, but the vast majority who had much contact with whites did. The courageous ones who didn't accept were rarely "successful," and often joined the ranks of the nearly, or the newly, dead.

When white society allowed Blacks to have their own "leaders," they were almost always white-appointed, hand-picked house niggers. It is interesting, but not surprising, to note that many of America's early Black leaders were often very fair-skinned and straight-haired individuals—the proud progeny of the slave masters. The Blacks who had the field nigger attitudes and status were seldom on intimate terms with the real engineers and controllers of the American society. They spent most of their time struggling to survive on the lowest economic level. Though they were forced to submit to whites as were their more "refined" brothers, the main difference in field and house niggers was that the former usually acquiesced for survival's sake, while the latter often accommodated for the purpose of material gain, as well as for the cause of practical survival. The popular designation of "Uncle Tom," after the publication of Harriet Beecher Stowe's famous novel, became a symbol for Black submissiveness and smiling docility. This designation, like so many other popular symbols in American life, tended to misrepresent and generalize a rather complex phenomenon.

Today, an "Uncle Tom" is openly ridiculed and scorned among Black people. He, or she (a female can be an "Uncle Tom" also, although she is often called an "Aunt Jemimah," or an "Aunt Jenny") is generally depicted as one who eagerly accepts and without apparent questioning goes along with the schemes of white folks. Also, the "Uncle Tom" is often pictured as one who "sells his people out" for his own personal interest. Such was not the case in the days of the legend's beginnings. An "Uncle Tom" was a Black person who was submissive and seemingly placid, occasionally even happy in the face of white supremacy. There were little, or no, overtones of actual betrayal or self-aggrandizement on the part of the Tom; he acted the way he did because he wanted to survive. In light of this basic definition, indeed most Black people became Uncle Toms, i.e., they assumed the strategy of survival in a hostile white world. This particular definition of Uncle Tom is similar to the presently popular understanding of what a Negro is. A valuable question now might be: just how many Black people are still Negroes/ Uncle Toms? or since both terms can be used as intransitive verbs, how many of them are yet negroing and tomming? And why?

The literary character on which the contemporary shameful figure is loosely based is very unlike his namesake. Stowe's Uncle Tom was presented as a truly magnanimous person of courage and principles. His spiritual strength and sense of integrity caused him to choose death rather than betray his people. He was a "decent" man who had, at least, one considerable fault —he believed in, and acted upon, the naive assumption that the people surrounding him had moral consciences. To be sure, he was not hostile to whites, nor, however, was he a dissimulator. The characters Quimbo and Sambo were actually treacherous, white worshippers, and indulged in self-serving interests at the expense of other Black people whom they brutalized. If labels and designations are important, the causes of clarity and analysis might better be served if not all Blacks who assume a practical survival posture are bunched together; perhaps they might be categorized according to their specific practices, if not their designs. Perhaps too, the appropriate and helpful names of Quimbo, Sambo, Negro and Tom might then be employed. The best response, of course, would be to end the necessity for these tactics.

In actuality, neither clarity nor analysis was used to deal with the image and reality of Uncle Tom. In their places, "militancy" was unleashed as a reaction to Uncle Tomism and elevated as one of the chief virtues of Black life. A number of Blacks began to gain a degree of respect from some of their fellows by casting off their white accruements—they not only rejected much of white aesthetic culture and its criteria for propriety, but they unashamedly returned to their African and field nigger heritages. (Because many of them did not know the differences, they confused the two.) They did not want to look, talk, nor act white. Some of them began to see the racial problem from a different position—the Black man in his "uncouth" state was no longer at fault; it was the "cracker" or "honkie" who was the hypocritical culprit.

The Black militancy that became popular in the 1960s resulted in and from many factors: the emergence of the "independent" African states in the late 1950s and early 1960s, and the prominence of some of their members in the U.N.; the rebellions in the ghettos; the postures of Robert Williams, R.N.A., the Deacons for Defense, and R.A.M.; the direct action of some of the civil rights organizations, specifically CORE, SNCC, and SCLC, the latter under the leadership of Dr. Martin Luther King, Jr.; the teachings and values of the Nation of Islam under the leadership of the Honorable Elijah Muhammed, especially as articulated by Malcolm X; and later, the unifying attempts of Ron Karenga's U.S. organization and the aggressive stance of the Black Panther Party. Even if many Black people did not always understand and embrace the fine points and analysis of the "problem" as offered by the above-named organized groups, they did accept their covert and overt pride and militancy. Militancy was definitely in (along with its gradual perversion)!

In the face of a long tradition of white arrogant handling and abuse of Black people, and much servile and disgraceful acquiescense on the part of official Negro leadership, the new militancy was a positive and necessary thing. It served for some as an important phase on the road to Black mental health, autonomous criticism, thought, and action; but for too many others it became the summum bonum of Black existence. Along with a resurgence of Black pride, the related militancy, for a time, had a positive influence on the people. Not only did militancy inspire them to seriously challenge many of the blatant insults from the overbearing white society, but a few also received the impetus and power to actually take on the societal mechanisms behind them. Its clarion call awakened and inspired many oppressed peoples throughout the nation and the world and, for a while, traumatized American society and frightened its government.

The major problem which arose with the Black militant posture was that it was seized upon by white foes and Black opportunists alike and perverted into little more than a mindless vehicle for blinding emotional orgasms. For too many people, militancy became an end in itself, a panacea which did not want or need Black original, critical, and creative thinking or thinkers. Being "outspoken" (even when one had nothing to say) and unsmilingly cold became cool. Methodology was but gray smoke to roaring Black rhetoric. For some people, signifying, wolf-ticketing, and cussing "whitey" took on high, significant Black cultural dimensions. Many militant Blacks not only publicly "told the cracker off," but they were most merciless in condemning Uncle Toms and the Black bourgeoisie house nigger (even when they didn't know what one was). The once despicable field nigger had now arrived—"field niggerism" was revived. Whereas a few years earlier many Black people wanted to be light and proper, if not white and right, now they desired to be Black, soulful, and some even wanted to be funky!

Had the characteristics of the newly projected blackness (soulfulness, and funkiness) served as genuine antidotes to and options for whiteness—that is, the sociopolitical oppressive force —the thrust of field niggerism indeed would have made a valuable contribution to Black (and white) life. In the main, the much heralded standards of blackness were little more than the old criteria of whiteness; both were grounded in American values. Both accepted a world view wherein the economically related notion of race, with its convenient correlatives, superior races, inferior races, racial hatred, etc., was unquestioned. Both rejected humane communal consciousness for irrational mob psychology. The main difference was that Black expressions were more exaggerated and emotional than their white counterparts. Instead of refuting white racist notions, muddled thinking, and actions, unthinking Black ideologists challenged the Caucasian monopoly and demanded their share (10 percent) of the American mess. While assuming the role of defensive racism, many Blacks denied the possibilities that Black people could be racists. Black racism, which has no power to impede and injure politically stronger whites, is a desperate and weak reaction to harsh Caucasian control. Moreover, it is misplaced. Since Black people are not able to institutionalize their bigotry in the manner of whites, their victims are almost always other Black people, the individual locked in the unprotected, already overly exploited Black ghetto.

In addition to appropriating racism and racial hatred and weaving them into the fabric of blackness, the purveyors of the new niggerism also ventured into the areas of aesthetics and ethics. Unfortunately for the Black community, they didn't go far enough into either and failed to distinguish the intricacies of the two. Ostensibly rejecting the long standing white claim that black was ugly and bad, the field folks avowed that, in reality, black was beautiful and good. Other Blacks, of course, were also saying that black was a positive entity, but it remained for the raucous new souls to cheapen and obfuscate its thrust. Excesses such as petty chauvinism, defensive racism, and intense herd (non) thinking perhaps were inevitable in the light of white historical suppression of Black life. The tragedy was that these excesses were elevated at the expense of sound thinking and allowed to operate as Black norms. Thus, a popular deformed blackness evolved that, while purporting to condemn white supremacy, actually embraced its anti-Black nature and designs, hence excluding creative and independent Black thinking.

Stunted blackness spread its contagion of irrationality and

irresponsibility throughout the Black community. Black individuals who had the perception to see and the courage to criticize the dangerous ethnic idiocy were bitterly attacked. The Black bourgeois leadership, true to its uncreative, craven character, either attempted to sidestep the wave of the new black foolishness or else they expediently rode the tide. Black was definitely beautiful and above question! Formerly designated bad hair, dark skin, and other "negative negroid" physical features were now seen in a complimentary light. A fascinating extrapolation was soon made by the thug section of the Black community; it reasoned that if blackness were indeed beautiful, good; and above criticism, all actions that emanated from Black people (the field variety in particular) would also be right (on). Hence, the bullying, slandering, extorting, exploiting, and even killing of Blacks by Blacks could continue, even escalate, with impunity.

Disavowing any allegiance to the laws and projected morality of white America, the opportunistic thuggish Black element, in effect, worked paw in claw with the most rabid white supremacists by renouncing all respect for and responsibility to other Black people. Entering in league with embittered, hate-filled, desperate Black men and women, the shady element attempted to present nonsense and neurosis as the correct, highest forms of blackness. A Black victim of this bogus blackness who criticized and sought restitution for a wrongdoing was condemned as an Uncle Tom and an enemy of the Cause. With the strong harassment and near total silencing of autonomous Black voices, accomplished by both the powerful white authority and its near illiterate field nigger henchmen, Black people, at large, stumbled in confusion and disarray. The Black bourgeois minions of white supremacy maintained their usual strategy and unquestioningly parroted, what appeared to them to be, the in-thing and attempted to turn it to their personal advantage.

The genuine interest and important involvement in Black culture as the phenomenon of militancy itself, too often became misused by certain shortsighted Blacks and manipulated by economically motivated whites until both "soul" culture and Black militancy were prevented from achieving their vast potentials. Merchants began to appropriate many artifacts, aids, and symbols of Black culture and began to mass-produce them. Dashikis, bubas, sandals, and Swahili were in. Even certain members of the Black bourgeoisie admitted that they liked "soul food"; a few actually acknowledged that they had tasted "chitterlings." Proper folks who up to this time had barely been able to manage a whispered "crap" were yelling "muthafuka" in public, straining for the right intonation. The funky butt had come of age. Johnny Mathis and the late Nat King Cole were all right, but it was the time for "Bloods" to get down. James Brown, who had already had appreciative fans (remember, "Please, Please, Please"?), was recognized as the official king. He was soul brother number one and he responded by assuring his subjects that he had the "feeling" and he was "Black and Proud," etc.

The bourgeois Black press (and its cohorts), as usual, was late getting into the act, but when it did it jumped in with a vengeance. It provided new Black successes (à la the old white patterns), the most popular Black leaders (i.e., entertainers, middle-class auxiliaries), new Miss Black and Afro-American beauty contestants, ad infinitum. Following the example of their white counterparts, models, and sometimse sponsors, middle-class members (and occasionally those who aspired to that fellowship) expertly wrote books on the timely subject-object. Their outpourings conjured up reminiscences of the 1920s' "Negro Renaissance," or worse. The crucial problem with the new "explosion of Blackness" was neither in its initial inspiration nor in its good intentions (on the parts of many individual Black people), but in the fact that it too quickly became stunted, exploited, and directed by alien and moneyed interests.

The hip, "now" Brother and Sister kept in fashion with merchandise made in Italy, Japan, Hollywood and from the ultra-chic storehouses of organized crime. The pattern of gross commercialization of the marketable aspects of Black culture is similar to the course travelled by the "natural" hairstyle. The people who were the first to wear their hair *au naturel* in the early 1960s and even up to 1967 (especially the women) were criticized, ridiculed, and on a few occasions spat upon. One can only imagine that people who subjected themselves to such abuse must have been very serious and knowledgeable about what they were doing. In time, the natural, or Afro, became accepted; "everybody started wearing it." The hairsyle evolved: it became longer, bushier, and efficiently groomed. It came in all colors, but by far the most popular kind was the bouffant type that was worn by Blacks with "good hair." Indeed, everybody started doing it— Black entertainers, undercover agents, preachers, prostitutes, policemen, the sons and daughters of the holdout coloreds, career soldiers, white Europeans, etc. They all were Black and proud, or, at least proud (well, they were fashionable)! As the co-option of the Movement continued, a contingent of hustlers were catapulted forward as spokesmen. Attempts were made to squelch authentic voices.[3]

Militancy often became a stylized way to blow off steam, impress some still cautious Blacks, and engage in harmless but sometimes profitable games with pseudoguilty white liberals. Hating whitey was rarely the same thing as hating whitey's logic, values, or goals. Seeing the counterproductive aspects in unthinking Black militancy, some slick whites seized upon it in order to "make a buck" and mollify some angry, frustrated niggers in the process. If the "new" pop Black leaders were occupying much of their time (when they weren't surviving and listening to soul music) in being "militant," they would have little occasion to critically think through, assess, plan, and organize. A particular negative element in the new militancy, especially among light-skinned bourgeois nationalists, was that it often led Black people to fight among themselves as to who, or what group was the *Blackest,* and who and what group had the canon and criteria for for orthodox *Blackness.* Plainly, people who are so involved can be of no real threat to their white oppressors, or comfort to their Black fellow victims.

Certain antagonists disrespected and bitterly attacked Blacks who disagreed with their pontifications and made great shows of openly exhibiting their personal infallibility and irresponsibility.[4] Similar characteristics had always appeared in Black communities throughout America, but in the 1960s they were modernized and renamed—the features, now parading under the labels, "Bad," "Cold," and "Black," for generations had simply been called stupidity. Black Militancy, that started out so gloriously and promised so much, in the main, degenerated into a diversion. The continuing tendency toward strong negative kind of Black militancy in the 1970s is based on three factors: (1) Entrepreneurial strategy; (2) Black naive and/or opportunistic reactions; and (3) the Black bourgeoisie mentality, especially among many young "middle-class" Black students.

Entrepreneurial strategy: it is, of course, to the advantage of the people in power if exploited Blacks do not truly understand the nature and the mechanisms of their own plight. By remaining in political ignorance and dissipating energies in ritualistic militancy, people cannot construct the effective tools essential for their liberation. Not only will the oppressed go around in circles, but certain exploiters will make money on their trips by selling them "natural combs," "hip garbs," "soul records," and movies and books whose major themes engage Black audiences in nonproductive chauvinism.

Black naive and opportunistic reactions: Black people who operate with a brand of defensive militancy, which purposely excludes critical thinking, are doing a disservice to the Black community. Even if they are sincere, the tactic of condemning their Black opposition and hating and castigating whitey does not aid in freeing Black people. One, of course, can generally villify, berate, and curse all Negroes and whites and worldwide whiteness, but such denouncements do not serve to expose nor lessen the power that even one alien radio station, publisher, policeman, or slum lord wields over the people. Perhaps some Black "militants" do not realize this truth; obviously, some of them do. In certain quarters, stunted Black militancy is a business that produced some meager social and financial rewards for its Black practitioners.

Black bourgeoisie mentality: perhaps the most tragic element among those who inadvertently embrace this reactionary tactic is an important section of Black youth. Being particularly incensed at historical Uncle Tomism, and often personally embarrassed and angered at the antics of their own accommodating middle-class parents, many of the bourgeois students highly esteem Black militancy and revere, at least in theory, the concept of the field nigger. They see Black militancy as a repudiation of white culture, and the field nigger as the ideal Black, free of all, or most, negative white values. Such a view is very simplistic, as it does not deal with the real complexities of white or Black life. (But curiously enough, the campuses and the streets of the nation are expert at encouraging both future radicals and hopelessly romantic reactionaries.)

In his intense response to organized oppression (exclusion?), the Black bourgeois youth often confuses certain potentially positive human scientific levers with white tools. Often, the invaluable instruments of self-discipline, and education itself, are equated with "white tricknology" and summarily rejected. Essential human discipline is sometimes considered the same thing as middle-class, insipid white propriety, and the systematic cultivation of the spirit and the mind is confused with white exploitative miseducation. Too often, autonomous and critical thinking on the part of a serious Black person is suspect. "Thinking Black" does not mean "thinking white," but it should not mean thinking small, or not thinking at all. Often in their guilt, resulting from the actions (or inactions) and class status of their parents, many Black bourgeois university students uncritically accept and romanticize the field nigger and field niggerisms generally. But just as guilt did not significantly help white liberals, it cannot help Black ones. To be sure, most aspects of the Black bourgeois person's life are stunted and noncreative because they are based on imitations of white models. In addition, much of his formal education has prepared him for a place carved by white supremacist paternalism. The Black bourgeois mentality must be criticized in a very severe but helpful manner and, if possible, finally healed. Perhaps it would do some good to exchange the house nigger mind-set for the present-day field nigger's mentality, but that transformation alone would likely be insufficient for freedom.[5]

No matter what the romantic contemporary version says about him, the field nigger too has suffered under the influences and manipulations of exploitative racist power. Even if he has not experienced the blight of the Black bourgeois class sham or undergone the ordeal of a higher, formal miseducation, he has been raised and trained in America. He knows firsthand many of the loyalties, priorities, and values of the privileged class through his radio, television set, and the movies. He often is, in his own unsophisticated and unpretentious way, greatly enamored of corrupting values. This especially holds true for the individuals about twenty-five years old and under who were raised on the claptrap of mendacious tv and white-supremacy-based, vampiristic integrated elementary education. Sometimes, the field nigger worships vaunted material possessions even more intensely than some of his house brothers simply because he has never had them and, hence, has never seen how worthless they really are.

Another very regrettable aspect of the return to field niggerism on the part of many Black people is that realistic and effective evaluations of Black life-styles are sacrificed in the cause of myopic chauvinism. Often, pimps, prostitutes, petty thugs, and one would assume (in order for the fledgling aficionado to be consistent) drug pushers are considered the new "Black heroes and heroines." They are so depicted because they "do not play by the white man's rules"; "they actually turn their backs on society's so called morality" and "fool whitey at his own game." The people who depend upon such heroes might as well whistle "oga bogum" in half time and beat three sticks together. This rather enthusiastic appraisal of the new Black "outsiders" does not take into consideration the very real fact that the heroes and heroines almost always demonstrate their independence within the tight confines of the harried Black ghetto and usually at the expense of its already exploited inhabitants. Perhaps these celebrated field niggers do not play by the most common set of whitey's rules, but obviously "Charlie" has other more binding sets that even the field folks don't violate—sets that, nevertheless, rigorously reinforce Black "inferiority" and white "superiority." Knocking over Mas and Pas, cutting Buba's throat, putting Baby Sister on the ho's stroll, and pushing junk are hardly in the same league with overthrowing a government or building a nation.

It is, of course, correct, I think, that many present-day Blacks do not consider the field outsiders as criminals nor condemn them as such. Not only are many of them "as good" as "normal law-abiding" people—some of them are better—but most of them are also attempting to survive oppressive social conditions in the best manner that they can. The word *criminal* is not an accurate description of them. (In one sense, however, Black people are criminals, since none are full citizens in the land of their birth, and all are pragmatically treated as wrongdoers; some are in maximum security prisons, while others inhabit minimum security institutions.) The unruly field nigger who, without radical design, skill, or direction, rebels against white authority should not be considered and labeled as a criminal, even if he is behind bars— generally, his little antics are childish Sunday-school exercises when compared to the machinations of the arch-societal criminals—nor, however, should he automatically be promoted as an instant cultural hero and an example for the children, especially if he is behind bars. (Both he and they must be taught that Black people have no business in white prisons.)

Attempts must also be made to understand and work with those few who might decorate their sloppy thugism with political rhetoric and flashy life-styles. Many Blacks who elevate the "outside of the law" field niggers often mistakenly point to Malcolm X as proof of their theory. In effect, they laud undisciplined roguishness. The man did not make significant contributions to the general Black human cause just because he had once been a "petty crook" and had spent some time in a white maximum security prison. He was able to be effective because he was a very gifted human being. The authenticity of Black life had not been beaten out of him, even by the cruel and self-destructive cycle inherent in the Black ghetto. Rather, it was kept alive by the love of his mother, the memory of his Garveyite father, and finally the enforced discipline of incarceration, the liberating teachings of the Honorable Elijah Muhammed, and by his own intrinsic desire to know, to be, to grow, and to serve. The celebration of petty thugism, nickel slickness, and poverty-producing desperation is foolish and irresponsible. It should never be confused with the actions of those concerned about the people who knowingly challenge the oppressors and their system.

The current elevation of the field nigger and general field niggerism are plainly recidivistic, a regression to the "good old days" when life was simpler and one did not have to organize or object to the powerful and complex forces of exploitation. Such a posture that refuses to see the real situation as it is cannot hope to come to grips with it, nor hope to change it. It is understandable but dangerously romantic. The oppressed can attempt to evade the actual causes of the daily crimes done against them, but none can escape their terrible and sure manifestations. Black will not be saved by the shouting of truncated militancy in public, the use of "Black English" in the schools, the bodies of Black prostitutes in the slums, drugs, alcohol, soul music, or the general projection of niggerism on the screen and in the streets. In order to become a freed people, clear, creative, critical, and autonomous thinking is needed, which, in turn, needs the sufficient political and economical power to support such thinking.

Genuine anger may help to trigger the people; nonreactionary culture can give them unity and direction; but political acumen and methodology are needed to bring about the victory. While it might not be necessary for Black people to get their bodies out of America, it is essential for them to get America (the cultural, social, moral catastrophe) out of their psyches. For too long, powerful, complex forces have caused many of the people to sleepwalk in unreflecting niggerhood. Real solutions will not be forthcoming from made-in-the-U.S.A. castes composed of stereotyped salty field niggers or moderate house niggers—but if it is to come, in the final analysis the definers and liberators will be Black human beings beyond both slave reflexes; they will be resurrected, redirected, unified, a world beyond mere pop militancy. It is time for the Black population in America to awake and come of age, even if America itself has not.

NOTES

1. During the late 1960s, the thrust and goals of the growing Black Movement conflicted with the designs of America's eco-

nomic system, the wishes of the F.B.I., under J. Edgar Hoover, and the aims of the new Richard M. Nixon Law and Order Administration, especially as they were spelled out by the President himself and his chief assistants, Spiro T. Agnew and John Mitchell.

2. A similar phenomenon appeared in other parts of the world wherever white authority ruled the lives of Black people. American de jure slavery started after the second decade of the eighteenth century and ended in 1863.

3. This strategy was effectively employed in American universities where cries for "relevant" education, more suited to the needs of human development than the schemes of the racist military-industrial complex, were raised. The Black and Ethnic Studies programs that initially promised to elevate "minorities," and the field of education itself, were designed to fail by school authorities who deliberately placed opportunists and politically inept individuals in leadership positions. People of principle and ability were almost always passed over.

4. For ample proof of this point, all one has to do is to check the many articles, pamphlets, poems, books, and speeches that were made during the period, especially up to Spring, 1968. Individuals who could not be trusted to deliver forty-four cents to an orphan home across the road at high noon or to muster the courage to face the welfare investigator were routinely and loudly slandering the great Dr. Martin Luther King, Jr., and other dedicated servants like him. People who would have been hard-pressed to organize a marble tournament were dispensing with the *only* strategy for the Movement and writing tracts on how to be *Black* in ten easy lessons.

5. To a degree, field niggers were and are, no doubt, more psychologically free and healthier than their domesticated brothers. A small number among the group of field niggers are actually the true daring Black existentialists, the so-called "crazy niggers"—Blacks so "wild" and independent of spirit that neither Black folks nor whites are able to control or comprehend them. This group, even to this day, has yet to be adequately depicted in literature.

ARE BLACK PEOPLE
(AND OTHER NON-WHITES)
AMERICANS?

Getting at the simple truth of any matter is not nearly as simple as it sounds, especially if the matter under investigation is as controversial and complicated as the status of African descendants in the United States of America. To bluntly answer either yes or no to the question of Black people's citizenship in the land of their birth would be misleading; conditions and qualifications would have to be introduced in both cases. To ask, why would a Black person wish to be an American citizen, might be an incisive response, but it would not come to grips with the question at hand. An American (i.e., a citizen either at birth or by naturalization) is a person of whom it can be said has the political and cultural rights and privileges of his nation. Do Black people have the rights and privileges that are guaranteed to citizens of America?

America is not a land, but a political/cultural entity, which evolved from a segment of the eighteenth-century Western European mind. The entity that was forcibly superimposed on the New World in time became highly structured and institutionalized. The original inhabitants of the land, now mistakenly called "Indians" (wrongly named by a European who thought he was on the subcontinent, India), are native to the land that the European invaders appropriated, but they are definitely not "native Americans." By claiming to be native Americans, the aborigines of the stolen continent would not only unwittingly give credence to the American system, but inadvertently accept their own displacement by that system. Thus, it is one thing to declare that the land now called America should belong to the Indians, who were there first; it is quite another thing to say that Indians are the true Americans. European white people, alone, are the true Americans.

To state that the oppressed Indians once owned the land, and the exploited Black people worked and built it up does not settle the question of American citizenship or its present ownership. America, as an institution, was designed by and for Europeans. Though both Red and Black people, as well as other non-whites, contributed to its growth, strength, and ideas, the American nation was never meant to be a place for freedom, justice, and equality for non-Europeans. Indians have generally been seen as obtrusive, exotic relics from the past. (They have been publically depicted as romanticized savages, when they have been depicted at all.) Black people, for the most part, have been projected and used as a labor device and as scapegoats. Other non-white people in America, either because of their slight number and/or their nonthreatening posture and assimilationist policies, have been tolerated as strange pets or adjuncts to the national work force. No matter who did or does its actual physical labor, fights its wars, defends and supports its way of life, and believes in and loves its government, the American system was made and yet operates for the benefit of the true American (white European) people.

Blacks and other "minorities" (they are only minorities to themselves if they see the rest of the world, where they are a part of the majority; that is, the minority classification is from a programmed American perspective) may say that they are indeed American citizens, who have not as yet received all of their guaranteed benefits. They certainly have a right to this view, which is, as they interpret it, buttressed by a semisacred piece of paper, i.e., the (white) American Constitution; but they should realize that America's past history, and its present day economics and politics are in direct conflict with their opinion. America's minorities, i.e., Afros (African descendants in the United States) and other Third World people, can attempt to ignore their true statuses as auxiliaries and functional tools, or else they can try to convince themselves that one day "things" will change. A significant change in their situation, however, would demand radical changes in both the political and cultural realities of America. It is a gross illusion to think that white supremacy and economic exploitation are mere aberrations, and not at the very center of American life. The American institution would never have been founded, nor could it continue its present course, without the active, effective presence of white racism and economic exploitation. As long as Americans operate with their present world view, their self-congratulatory and self-deluding understanding of America's nature, purpose, and influence, they will continue to help produce and need disorganized, politically weak minorities, i.e., "niggers," "red savages," "greasers," "chinks," et al.

In the main, then, it is a weighted risk for Black and other oppressed people to persist in appealing to the Courts, the Constitution (who will do the interpreting, if not individuals with Americanized white mentalities?), and to the general conscience of America. It borders on unmitigated stupidity for them to embrace and live by America's standards of culture, patriotism, and morality. They will not make human advancements. They will not be admitted as first-class Americans because of their loyalties and actions, nor will they remove the onus of "inferiority" from themselves. Their's is a delegated inferiority,[1] presented to them by whites in authority who wanted to justify, rationalize, and enforce their system. The primitive-based psychic disease and economic tool of racism, "racial inferiority" (and its companion, "racial superiority"), is religiously embraced, used, and reinforced by average whites who benefit from the unjust, criminal system, of which they are a willing, if unenlightened, part. At this time in history, a nine-year old child should be able to see through the charges of, and rationales for, racial inferiority on the part of degenerate criminals who seek to demean, demoralize, disarm, as well as to exploit, their victims. Oppressed people would do well to go beyond the stages of proclaiming that "they are as good as the white man," and that they are in fact "beautiful." Both declarations might help to ward off boredom on a rainy afternoon, but they represent a position that too easily leads to political diversions.

People are not oppressed because they lack "goodness"— moral or general human; nor are they oppressed because they are not "beautiful." People are not even oppressed because they fail to make an impressive score on an "official, objective" test for abstract intelligence. People who are oppressed owe their plight to their disorganized and politically weak state. Conversely, oppressors are not better, lovelier, nor brighter than their victims (though they are, in every case, more unscrupulous and amoral); but they are more politically organized. For Black people to continue to play white racist games, by appealing to their sense and structures of justice and by remonstrating their own intrinsic value, is to court folly. To say that "we are essentially citizens (because we were here before the Mayflower, or that we've earned citizenship, or that we produce great musicians, etc.) though not practically treated as such" is to enter into a curious word exercise whose conclusions lead one to say nothing at all.

If Black people in America are not Americans, what are they? To be sure, most of them are African by recognizable ancestry, and some of them are African by sentiments and deeply felt, well-thought-out loyalties. In spite of the official Western positions, many Black people in the New World also have retained numerous Africanisms,[2] which are evident in their approaches to life and in their culture. But, of course, Black people who are thousands of miles and centuries from the African continent cannot be said to be Africans in a legal sense. This is not to say that they cannot become legally Africans. Africans, leaders and nonleaders alike, even as late as the prelude to the twentieth century, publically wondered when were their people "coming back home."[3] It now remains for both interested Afros (or New World Africans) and Africans to enter into dialogue concerning a Black exodus, and its particulars.

To be sure, there will be many, perhaps the majority of New World Africans, who cannot, or will not desire to move to the African continent. All, at least, should have the knowledge that they are not Americans. It is high time that people stop deluding themselves. If they become realistic in their understanding of what America is and what it is not, they will be free to realize exactly what constitutes an American. With the present, actual definition, supported and reinforced by the reality of politics, non-whites are not Americans. (While they are not eligible to fully participate in the material benefits of America, they can fall prey to its chief disadvantage, materialism.) They are wards, victims, possessions, and tools of America. Only white people can be Americans, and even the average white can be a simple citizen; he has no power to govern America or to direct his own destiny in it. One day, interested Black people and other non-whites might be able to transform themselves into biologically white individuals (they have already devised a way to reconstruct their minds into the white image), but until that time comes they would do well to adopt other alternatives.

One alternative that is open to all oppressed people is to be content with their oppression. If they are occasionally displeased with the roughest edges of their plights and, in spite of themselves, entertain intermittent desires for freedom, they might commission their best minds, not to lead them to freedom, but to make their slavery more comfortable and replete with fantasy. Whites in authority will be only too glad to sponsor, promote, and finance such leaders. Another alternative is to enter into a union with other like minds and spirits in order to liberate America; Black people will never be politically free in America until America itself is free. Just as there now are strict cultural and political boundaries between being an American and being Black, there are stricter boundaries—cultural, political, and spiritual—between being an American and being a free human being. America is not a land, but a political/cultural entity, an eighteenth-century institution with many modern technological advantages and many primordial moral weaknesses, an old idea whose time has passed. America needs to be reclaimed and renamed by the people, for the good of a common humanity.

NOTES

1. Components constituting "inferiority" are derived from the biblical Hamitic curse, perverted Calvinism, and social Darwinism.
2. These characteristics, properly understood and developed, should assist in leading the people to a fuller, freer future, and not into the clutches of a beguiling mistake of living in a (psychological) museum even if it is an African one.
3. *See* Bishop Henry McNeal Turner's account in *African Letters* (Nashville: A.M.E. Sunday School Union, 1893).

JUSTICE AS SUBVERSION

White supremacy, or the devastating, racist self-serving device of the "white race," is installed both in the political-economic structure, and in formal and informal educational systems of modern society. All white people receive material benefits from it, while all non-whites are, in varying degrees, penalized and exploited by white supremacy. The whitest white folk (the Anglo-Saxons) are highest in the category of valued people, while American Indians (sic) and the world's Blacks occupy the lowest. It matters little that the Anglos constructed the categories and appointed the places themselves, since for the last five hundred years, few people have seriously challenged the arrangement. Most of the other non-Anglo Caucasians, especially the off-white groups, e.g., the Italians, Greeks, Spaniards, Slavs, et al, generally help to guarantee the top spot for the Anglos as they religiously lay claim to their related, secondary pale statuses.

The "mixed" races (hybrids of white sires and non-white female slaves) almost always haughtily alienate themselves from their darker half-siblings in favor of the crumbs that fall from the tables of their master-relatives. As a people, Western Jews, a group of obscure background,[1] though in many ways more politically able than the Anglos themselves, illustrate their dedication to Anglo racial superiority by insisting that they are good standing members of a category that has degraded and oppressed them for centuries.[2] The Japanese, in the main, act as a curious force within the sphere of racism. While they surely are not white in any racial sense, the Japanese establishment's acceptance and adherence to the ethics of Angloism conveniently qualify them as honorary white people. They are so listed in South Africa.

There is no question about Black people; they are consigned to the bottom—the furthest distance from Anglos. Constant and massive attempts are made to insure that their actual predicament reflects their stratification. Almost all of the other colored groups of the world derive their meaning and places in society by staying as far away from Black people as they can.[3] The white device, and the divide and conquer strategy that comes from it, have been so successful that actual white presence is not needed to assure their continuation and efficacy. Colored people of the world exist in a state of disorganization and weakness owing to Caucasian manipulation. They also contribute to their own plight by emulating and accommodating white racist philosophies and ideas, and by deserting their own values.

To say that all white people benefit by white supremacy is not to say that they are all bigots. White supremacy is so entrenched in our present age as to be as constant and unwavering as the sun rising in the east and setting in the west. The white individual who would see it in all of the enormity of its accumulative horror would have to be a near genius; he would have to approach sainthood in order to completely repudiate the advantages of white supremacy and to be content with just being a human being. In the present order of things, the lowest, most stupid, most immoral white person has cultural myths, social securities, and political reinforcements that convince him that he is better than the most noble non-white human being. Crimes of the most infamous nature have been done, are being committed, and will be perpetrated against non-whites by whites who use the rationales and presuppositions of white supremacy. Whites, even "good whites," seldom attack white supremacy, and they rarely attack it at its core, with inspired conviction and vigor.

The recent public cry that "Black is beautiful" partially indicated that many Black people privately suspected that it was just the opposite. No matter how worthy individual Blacks feel themselves to be, they unmistakably recognize the powerful, demonic cultural and political forces arrayed against their race. Though "Black is beautiful" was, in part, a cry of compensation and a whistling in, and for, the dark, it was a big improvement over the past slogan: "I'm just as good as the white man!" Obviously, as long as white was the acceptable value criteria,

Blacks still had to confront the total ideological foundation for white supremacy as well as the political-economic base for the criminal device. Blacks, Asians, and other Third World people have indeed made progress, and though political revolution could easily topple the forces of white supremacy, it is almost a certainty that the destructive device will be ended by the liberation of the mind and the spirit.

White supremacy was constructed by people; it can and will be destroyed by people. Millions of whites live in real fear that their uncooperative victims will one day awake, unite, and seek vengeance. The third response does not necessarily have to follow the first two. People who desire authentic freedom rarely have the time or interest to wish for new masters and slaves, or new superior and inferior colors. True liberty and true justice for all people are their goals. However, in light of the undeserved power and stolen wealth that whites have wielded for centuries, it is not too difficult to understand why they fear the advent of universal freedom and justice. If chronic white supremacists could not rule, exploit, and murder millions of people with impunity, they could not survive. They will not survive. Justice is slow in coming to full bloom, but it is a truth that will outlast white supremacy. It will outshine the sun.

NOTES

1. Arthur Koestler, *The Thirteenth Tribe: The Khazer Empire & Its Heritage* (New York: Random House, 1976).
2. Perhaps as a reaction to Adolf Hitler's reading them out of the white race, contemporary Jews tend to uncritically claim membership into that politically privileged brotherhood.
3. There are always exceptions in both groups and in individuals. Mexico's former president, Luis Echeverria, India's Indira Gandhi and the late Mao Tse-tung of the People's Republic of China have openly declared their solidarity with all oppressed peoples; so too, has Cuba, with Fidel Castro, and Sirimavo Bandaranaike of Sri Lanka.

THE BOOKER T. PROCESS—
MANIPULATION OF
BLACK LEADERS

During the 1960s, the long struggle for Black liberation reached its apogee in the United States of America. In that same period, it also started a perilous descent from which it has not recovered. Until that time, with the possible exception of Marcus Garvey's beleaguered and short-lived thrust of forty years earlier,[1] no major and/or national civil rights body had ever demanded actual power and self-sufficiency for Black people.

Mr. Booker T. Washington,[2] the earliest and best promoted national "Negro leader," set the stage for the substance, if not the struggle, for subsequent Black leadership in America. Basing his public stance and philosophies on his reading of the political and economic realities of late nineteenth-century America,[3] Mr. Washington attempted to get the best deal he could for the oppressed, unorganized Black populace by calling for a reasonable détente between unequals. He sought the favor of powerful white patrons, and a lessening of the active ill will from the white masses for the benefit of his people.

In line with his comprehension of the temper of the times and the state of general Black unpreparedness, Washington apparently reasoned that the majority of Black people would be much better off with some economic viability, agricultural and technical skills, and a negotiated truce with white oppressors, than they would in writing Shakespearian sonnets, learning classical Greek, and agitating for the right to vote. Though he had his critics, the young Dr. W. E. B. DuBois was one of the majority— the Tuskegee professor was the most respected and best established leader of his people, widely recognized by Caucasians and Blacks alike. Dr. DuBois did not deny Mr. Washington's right to lead; he, however, wanted to see the emergence of other Black leaders. DuBois also wanted Mr. Washington to alter his priorities.

Because Dr. DuBois was aggressive in his condemnation of legal racial segregation and very critical of Mr. Washington's blatant accommodationist policies, many younger Black people chose the Harvard trained scholar as their hero and example. Conversely, they consigned Mr. Washington to a position a notch or two above Judas Iscariot: he became known as the archetypical "Uncle Tom." Many Black people after the time of Dr. DuBois, who considered themselves activists and militants, wrongly placed DuBois and Washington in separate camps and misread the former's position while ignoring the latter's.

During the period in which their debate was waged, the two men differed in style, approach, and rhetoric, hardly in substance. Nonetheless, innumerable people have since allowed themselves to become locked in an either/or situation on their stances.[4] From 1915, the time of Mr. Washington's death, until the 1950s, no one took the professor's place. Indeed, the intervening generation witnessed a long slow process of litigations for the rights of Black people. The NAACP, an integrated, largely Black-fronted organization, which sought support from white philanthropy, was in the forefront of "the struggle." Of course, there were publicized individual leaders after Washington's death, e.g., Dr. W. E. B. DuBois himself, Walter White, Mary McLeod Bethune, A. Phillip Randolph, Lester Granger, William Hastie, Ralph Bunche, Roy Wilkins, Bayard Rustin, and Whitney Young, but none of them approached the prominence or influence of Washington.

Until the 1950s, a few Black men had gained some national attention, but either because of their associations and their "ideologies," they were not given wide or favorable coverage. Paul Robeson and Richard Wright were two examples. Instead, the existing powers in America turned the spotlight on certain Black entertainers and athletes. Louis Armstrong, Bill Robinson, Hattie McDaniel, Joe Louis, and Jesse Owens, etc., were heavily promoted as Negro celebrity leaders. Whether or not they could or wanted to speak, they were projected as spokesmen for their race. Unfortunately, many Black newspapers and magazines uncritically accepted this celebrity leadership and are promoting them even to this day.[5] Thus a few promoted, generally apolitical individuals are pitted against sophisticated multinational corporations and power blocs.

Because Negro celebrities are almost always projected as important Black leaders by the powerful communications media, many leaders and would-be leaders aspire to celebrity status. Some Black individuals with real abilities are prevented from helping their people because they are tricked into useless egoism and deadend peer competition. Many more Blacks, those with messianic complexes and mosquito talents, actually do harm to Black people. In their foolish attempts to promote themselves as super-celebrities, they reinforce the white supremacist status quo and contribute to the further diminution of the masses of Black people. Obscured always in the glow of the starlight of the pampered Black entertainer-celebrity leader is the miserable plight of millions of his/her oppressed Brothers and Sisters.

In 1956, Dr. Martin Luther King, Jr., was catapulted into national promince with the Montgomery bus boycott, and in 1957, he became president of the newly formed Southern Christian Leadership Conference. Because he was a Baptist minister and an advocate of nonviolence, he was quickly seized upon by the white engineers and apologists for the American system as a shining celebrity, the new Booker T. Washington. (They had never understood the "old" Booker T. Washington, and in time, it would become evident that they would also misunderstand Rev. King.) Dr. King's direct action methods and soulful rhetoric only helped to add a little updated spice to the old accommodationist strategy. For a while, Rev. King was considered an ideal figure to forestall growing Black anger and inevitable progress because: (1) he didn't upset too many white liberals; (2) he tended to pacify many Blacks; and (3) he didn't constitute a concrete threat to established power in America.

The powerful people and groups in America did not count on the minister's integrity and his real dedication to the cause of

Black and oppressed people. They did not realize that, nudged along by crucial changes in the world, strident voices and strong national trends, and his own growing vision, Dr. King would begin to move away from a mere accommodationist stance. While Dr. King's transformation was occurring, another Black group emerged—the Nation of Islam. The Nation, under the leadership of the Honorable Elijah Muhammed, and the powerful voice of Malcom X, influenced Dr. King and a large segment of Black America.

Though the Nation of Islam had been around for about a generation, as a Black religious sect, it had received almost no national attention until the 1950s. Undoubtedly, the combination of Mr. Muhammed's then publicized principles and Malcolm X's charisma and quasi-political words frightened many average white Americans and excited many Black people. The power elite of America was uncertain if it constituted a real threat to the status quo. What they read as Muslim moralism, Black pep-talking, and reverse racism posed no real problems to them or to their hold on the actual world. They, however, continually cast the "Black Muslims" in a bad light as they realized the positive potentials in any independent Black organization. Malcolm's subsequent conflicts with the Muslims and especially his untimely death left the powerful white enclave briefly at ease. Both Malcolm X and Martin Luther King, Jr., were considered unpredictable activists who had to be monitored. No matter how aggressive and militant their rhetoric, as long as they did not effectively organize Black people to challenge the basic structure of society they were tolerated. Both men were assassinated, as they were widening the scope of the Black struggle, before they were able to implement any radical structural changes in America. However, they did leave their marks in the realm of ideas and values.

Many young leaders, spokesmen, militants, and revolutionaries followed Dr. King and Malcolm X, and though owing many of their ideas and insights to the two (especially to Malcolm X), they tried to outdo them in militant posturing and "Black" rhethoric. Though some were sincere, dedicated, and courageous, they generally made the mistake of confusing anger with understanding and rhetoric with organizing. For a few years during the 1960s, the mass media became fascinated with young militants, and while they were not looked upon as responsible or respectable leaders, they did attain a quasi-celebrity status. Some of the new militant celebrities made the mistake of becoming more interested in their new found status and the material benefits that might be derived from it than the needs of their followers. The loud cry was often "Black power," and later, "power to the people," while the quiet whisper actually directed benefits to individual pockets and egos.

A problem even more dangerous than the one of petty, individual opportunism was the manner in which the new leaders were controlled and manipulated by white interests. Under the banner of coalitions with "enlightened" American Caucasian hippies, clergymen, yippies, so-called socialists, etc., many young, untested, inexperienced Blacks entered the same old accommodationist relationships.[6] Only the Black militant and radical rhetoric were different; the substance of the unequal arrangement remained the same. In addition, many Black people bought the anti-Black unity propaganda of their Caucasian oppressors and began to redefine the word "Black" and the concept "Black power" in accordance with white interests. They either rejected the reality of Black altogether, or else they embraced a corrupted, white concept of Black.

The concept, "Black," was stripped of its spiritual and cultural foundation and implications (Black had served as a functional word for a community of people who had a common history from Africa to America) and became a reaction to the racial and racist term "white"; it became both dependent upon and subordinate to it. The necessary concept and goal of Black power, i.e., the attempt at community and personal self-definition, self-defense and self-development, was trivialized and reinterpreted as a call to Black hate, Black racism, and a stylized, empty Black militancy. Thugs, agents, charlatans and incompetents rushed in to assume positions as the new now Black leaders. Sinister and treacherous whites gladly sponsored and promoted these men and women, and highlighted their ridiculous antics and statements.

Too many Black people, those who accepted and those who rejected "Blackness" and "Black power," uncritically embraced the white, mass-media perverted, limited definitions. Thus the majority of the neo-leaders (local, and those who aspire to national influence), despite their touted modernity, celebrated militancy, and abrasive "field nigger" style, are in substance rank accommodationists. What they lack in understanding of the true nature of the American and Western societies, they more than make up for in their fantasizing and emotionalism.

Hence, Black people are still shamelessly divided, exploited, and blatantly oppressed, not because the masses of whites are stronger or smarter than they, but because from their historical amoral authoritarian position the ruling powers in the nation to outorganize and outmaneuver them. Blacks are kept in a state of political and psychic imbalance, and too many wear stylish masks to hide their desperation. The average, promoted, safe leader is especially devoted to deception. As a cowardly and greedy pawn in the hands of his white masters, he attempts to delude his followers, whose welfare he works against. This flunky leader actively plays his part in the silent but effective conspiracy to keep Black people demoralized, divided, and under the corrupt control of white supremacy.

The American ruling class fears Black spiritual, cultural, and mental autonomy, as well as organic unity among Black people. Blacks will never gain either autonomy or unity or the freedom that these desired goals could bring unless they begin to clearly see, strongly state, and honestly deal with the actual nature and ramifications of their real problems. Presently, the Black scattered communities are permeated with gross inferiorization and dependent, demoralizing slave values, which result in internecine envy and pettiness. If inferiorization and the vestiges of slave logic were eradicated among black people, Black oppression and exploitation would forthwith end.

Harold Cruse, in his valuable book, *Crisis of the Negro In-*

tellectual, offers important insights into the anti-Black environment that hems Black leaders in. Because they are politically
assimilationists and psychologically dependent upon Anglo and
Jewish authorities and propaganda, they do not work for the
benefit of Black people. According to Cruse, the leaders are not
in tune with Black nationalism. If his Black nationalism includes
concerns for Black dignity, autonomy, and freedom, I definitely
agree with him. My emphasis on Black leaders, however, differs
from his. The vast majority of promoted, recognized Black
leaders are either bought and paid for, petty, opportunistic crooks,
or else, shortsighted, ignorant puppets and, as such, deserve to be
understood, rehabilitated, and given bit parts on a Norman Lear
television show.

As Black people's political awareness increases, they will
recognize the folly in allowing others (especially members of
the groups that oppress them) to make and certify their leaders.
From this recognition, a communal atmosphere will result wherein authentic leaders will come to the fore, and sham leaders will
be exposed and properly rejected. Blacks will see the danger in
reacting piecemeal to constant oppression. Instead of throwing
together weak ad hoc groups to meet the sustained, murderous
attacks of long-standing organized institutions, the people will
understand the ongoing crisis of their predicament and prepare
themselves to confront and end it. Men and women of integrity,
foresight, imagination, and love will contribute to the community's
vision, unity, and effectiveness.

In time, the work and meaning of Booker T. Washington, as
well as the Black leaders who followed him, can be reevaluated.
Perhaps it will then be shown how similar they all were (and are)
except for one fundamental factor: it is likely that, at least,
Booker had a greater understanding of the nature of racist, capitalistic America than all of the other later leaders combined.
Black people in the United States of America, and indeed throughout the world, will be free when they can produce, recognize,
authenticate, sustain, and define their own leadership. The new
leadership will not be based on narrow, individualistic machinations nor celebrity quality (mistakenly labeled charisma), nor

will it reflect the designs of outsiders; but it will evolve from and for a people's strength and highest aspirations.

Oppressed people do not need pop heroes, heroines, and trendy idols as much as they need autonomous leaders who will place community welfare above self-aggrandizement. Individual gold medals and records, Academy Awards, athletic championships, Nobel and Pulitzer prizes, special recognitions, et al., lose their luster in the face of the multiple tragedy of Black people throughout the earth. The honors (especially most that come from the West) become a sham when Black people in Africa, the West Indies, North America, and in other parts of the world continue to supply entertainers, scapegoats, and assorted slaves to Western Europe and America. (Making or breaking a record, running with a ball, having a volume in "the book of the month club," or drinking coffee with a president have thus far not appreciably altered the circumstances of the majority of people in Kingston, Notting Hill, Harlem, or Soweto.)

The surest gauge for greatness in a leader is greatness in the people with whom he is associated. Greatness in both cases include freedom and human development. Great individuals die, but a strong united community grows and goes on.

NOTES

1. Universal Negro Improvement Association and African Communities' League of the World.
2. There were, of course, many local and regional leaders. Frederick Douglass (1817-1895), the abolitionist politician and editor, had national prominence, but not great national promotion.
3. Washington's policy was announced at the Cotton Exposition in Atlanta, Georgia, in 1895.
4. William Monroe Trotter (1868-1934), a contemporary of both Washington and DuBois, was more radical than either man, yet he received very little national attention during his time; he receives even less in ours.

5. Contemporary Black magazines are little more than slick organs for the feats, capitalistic life-styles, and muddled thinking of Black entertainers and athletes. Whites either own these publications outright or else control their contents through the tool of advertisement.

6. Also, by naively accepting the mass-media promoted foolishness of "not trusting anyone over thirty," they further severed themselves from their people and the wisdom of experience of their elders.

SHOULD SISTERS AND BROTHERS SUE THE WEST FOR ALIENATION OF AFFECTION?

The renowned Black scholar, Dr. W. E. B. DuBois, wrote in his book, *Darkwater,* that he could forgive the white slave masters for everything that they did to Black people, except for the utter humiliation that they inflicted on the African woman. By quoting an average white male detractor of Black femininity, Dr. DuBois was able to succinctly depict both the designation and the general treatment of the Black woman—"She's no lady; she's a nigger." Thus, the degradation of centuries is tied into that short symbolic sentence.

In spite of the fact that Dr. DuBois was unable to forgive the slave masters for their horrible assault on the Black woman, many Blacks, before and after the sage's time, have apparently been able to forget what Black women have been forced to undergo. There have been too few major programs that have attempted to deal with the many scars—cultural, mental, psychological, and spiritual—that the system of white racist Euro-America has had on her, and on the Black family and the relationships of Black women and Black men.

For a long time, Black leaders and organizations paid little attention to the special problems and needs of Black women. The era of political submission did not save them, nor did the periods of litigation, direct action, "Black Power," or the recent trek into the "Black Revolt." Black women were seized as spoils of war and brought to the New World as a commodity—Black women were used as producers of slaves. Hence, their worth was related to their anatomical makeup; if they knew how to use their equipment well they might be considered practical and valuable. From the beginning, the Black woman's role became shaped vis à vis her sex and around the needs of the white man. She was often required to minister to his sexual needs, and in other manual and menial capacities. The Black man, himself a captive commodity, was not able to save Black women from the white masters' authority.

In order to assure the continuation of the slave society—both the earlier de jure and the present de facto—certain men brutally and severely punished Black men for challenging their authority. Though their methods for dissuading Black men and penalizing them have changed, they yet retain one of their arch strategies in frustrating Black men and controlling the Black community: the manipulation of many Black women. Quoting a Muslim source, C. Eric Lincoln writes:

> This is no accident: the white man controls the economy, and he knows the Black Man is at his mercy. He deliberately castrates the Black Man by paying his wife higher wages, so that the male is no longer head of his family. The wife then comes to despise her husband and to admire the white man, who is economically independent.[1]

While the white male oriented society repressed the white woman, it did encase her into the pristine garbs of perpetual virginity; she was marked as a little, perfumed, pink pedestalized poodle, while the Black woman was designated as a musky, dusky alley bitch.

> By the hands of our white slave masters, we were reduced to a sub-human state, stripped bare of every ounce of intelligence and womanhood we've ever possessed. The Black woman's image has suffered greatly from being forced into a stereotype that has been passed down from slavery. This stereotype brands her as being the most

evil, ugly, and depreciated woman of all nations. It says
that she is physically unattractive . . . and good for nothing more than a convenient sex object, having babies and
working as a mammy in a white man's kitchen.[2]

Though ruling-class white men reduced Black women to
abject humiliation, they placed them on a higher level and in
opposition to the despised Black men. Black men were taken
from Africa for their slave labor. Since they were physically
stronger and apparently not as emotionally pliable as Black
women, Black men came under more physical abuse. Black men
were tyrannized and kept in "their place." Black women, because
they represented less of a threat to the slave system, were given
more latitude within the white supremacist context than were
Black men.

To be sure, all Black women did not relish or take advantage
of their status over Black men, but many of them inadvertently
made use of it. Forced conflicts and animosities arose. During the
time of de jure slavery, the women approximated some stability
and limited, derivative authority among Blacks. Since the period
of Reconstruction, the job market, albeit, often in menial capacities, has been more widely open to Black women than to Black
men, thus installing them as the authoritarian figure or the head
of the household. Some Black women, to this day, entertain
feelings of resentment and superiority to their male counterparts
because of the preferential treatment that they received from white
men. Added to these feelings is the attitude that certain Black
women have about themselves as highly desirable sex objects
(the earlier opprobrious societal designation has gradually re-
ceded until it has all but disappeared in the current, "Black is
Beautiful" phase).

Convinced that they have a going commodity, a good thing,
they affix high prices, taxes, and surcharges on it. The Black man
who can win the attention and favors—and if he is really successful, the hand—of such a woman rarely does so because of the
contents of his character or the depth of his love, but on the
amount of money he has and on the fashionable life-style he

exhibits. Since the showpiece woman thinks she is serving an important social function, she recognizes no real obligation to develop her personality or her mind. Indeed, all she needs in order to retain her market value are: (1) an attractive body; (2) an impressive array of stylish clothes; (3) a contingent of dilettantes —conditioned, shallow traffickers in the feminine façade; and (4) the continuation of a dehumanizing system that values acquisition, forms, and things over human beings.

Along with manipulating Black women, while cruelly exploiting them, white authority has also viciously manipulated and oppressed Black men. The denial of their ability and potentials as human beings (and as an active, successful man in this dog-eat-dog system) has forced Black men, by the thousands, to desert their families, turn to alcohol and drugs, to inhabit prisons, and occupy early graves. Plainly the failure of many Black men has not been a lack of desire for freedom for themselves and their people, nor in their moral and physical courage or strength,[3] but in their inability to organize Black people in the face of racist ubiquitous brutality, and the more dangerous skillful treachery. However, as noble as the struggle for liberty has been, and as savage and cunning as his oppressors are, the Black fighter for freedom has been charged with the specific onus of Black people's plight.

Many whites and a misguided number of Blacks, especially a showcase segment of captious Black females, are fond of saying that Black men are not at all men. They apparently confuse and equate the general Black man's lack of political power, and his inability to exploit people and accumulate money or materialistic junk, with the necessary human ingredients that make one a man. This charge on Black people's part is especially tragic since it serves to do three negative things: (1) it obscures the nature of the real problem; (2) it inevitably accepts and reinforces the elite white male's self-serving myths and his control of the Blacks; and (3) it precludes a vision that could lead Black people from white racist values and slavery to human values and independence. Capitalism (and human exploitation) is embraced, and the Black woman and man continue in a pernicious competition.

Today, many "experts," Black as well as white, simplistically proclaim that all Black women need are good, strong Black men, and everything will be all right! They fail to give their definition of "strong." Moreover, they announce "a nigger (i.e. Black man) ain't shit." While the ranks of Black men are being systematically decimated by America's foreign and domestic wars, i.e., inhuman penal institutions, drug culture, and the vicious human-destroying cycle inherent in the violent ghettos, the public is often glibly informed that Black men are genetic rascals, often "without balls," while Black women are the lonely "Queens of the Universe." One is never told where such information is obtained, who crowned the Black woman "Queen," and (most importantly) why. One does know that, while white folks have heroes, Black people are assigned heroines. An independent Black man is especially condemned and hated in a direct ratio to what extent he is feared. Thus, the various words of today converge to assure that structured white power will again avoid being recognized as the chief, if not the exclusive, cause of the plight of Black people. If "a nigger ain't shit" and is definitely "not a man," then by implication, it would seem that the "pecker-wood" is shit, a real "man," and our bright and shining model. In all of his accumulated preposterousness, he is the man model.

Intermittently, Black "experts," usually female spokesmen for the "Black woman's point of view," are trotted out by the mass media in order to deprecate Black men and undermine the rationale and necessity for the destruction of the status quo. Because they are heavily promoted, the opinions of these individuals assume quasi-sacrosanct proportions. The real problems of white racism, exploitative, monopolistic capitalism, militarism, and imperialism are all obscured, ignored, and replaced by the nationally more palatable issues of the amazing, amazonlike strength of the Black woman, deserted "welfarettes," the burgeoning ranks of Black feminists, and the male chauvinistic "ego" competition between white and Black men. It should not be surprising that many Blacks will swallow such bait, for in the minds of many of them, prominence and recognition in the white world still guarantees immediate celebrity status and leadership in the Black one. Whether a person is a sincere observer, a crass opportunist, or simply a naive, myopic individualist, she or he can be used to exploit the disastrous Black condition, and highlight and promote white, anti-Black values as well.

While Black males are being slaughtered in the Atticas, South Africas, Rhodesias, Vietnams, and in ghettos all over America, some naive Black women and feminized Black men, are being installed as leaders. Some of the system's most voracious "militant Black writers" find little good in Black men, but, when expedient, revere the Black "Queens." While I join those panegyric Black brothers in heralding the physical beauty and singing ability (many of the "Queens" are singers, though some of them are pinup girls in magazines and starlets in Hollywood) of certain Black women, I do not share their apparent belief that physical appearance and entertainment talent alone will help men or women achieve freedom.

In the past, Black women were not designated as human beings, but as sensual bodies. What good will it accomplish if, today, men shout that Black women are indeed "bodies," but glamorous ones? What are "glamor" and "pretty" but masks drawn from sterile stereotypes? Glamor, tuff naturals, big legs, $98.57 boots, and short skirts have little to do with being either human or free. Perhaps in addition to calling Black women beautiful "Queens," new criteria for beauty should be discovered or created that includes integrity, honesty, compassion, kindness, love, justice, and freedom. Increasingly white racist and materialistic values are taking their toll on Blacks—women as well as men. One might seriously question the Black fadlike phrase, "Black is beautiful," and the current secular vogue that witnesses Blacks calling each other "Brother" and "Sister" (in order to insure that they are more than fads and vogue). In America, though it is usually ranted over, color appears to be skin deep, while greed and exploitation are to the bone.

In the elitist white male's continuing attempt to maintain control and exploit the Black community, he makes the effort to feminize Black men and masculinize Black women. The popularity of Flip Wilson's "Geraldine" is, I think, not a coincidence.

The mass media, especially movies, television, and books, reflects the white male's interests. Black starlets galore, and an assortmen of femmes fatales of the "funky soul set" are constantly appearing in degrading roles on the "silver screen." Recently, some have been pushed as authoritarian saviors of pitiful Black people. Television projects a steady array of female starlet leaders. Black males who are presented are almost always apolitical athletes, vague entertainers, or "universal" comedians. White males are always "in the wings, pulling the strings," and setting the tone for Black "leadership" and "Black values." The Black masses are supposed to react properly, i.e., like damned fools.

The patterns of reaction and confusion were evident during the presidential compaign of 1972. Many Black people were uncertain as to how they should approach the candidacy of Congresswoman Shirley Chisholm of New York. Because she was Black, they were naturally attracted to her person and position; because she was a Black woman, they showed double interest. Those who refused to support her, or actually opposed her running, were considered by some of their fellows as preferring a white (George McGovern and Richard Nixon were the main candidates) to a Black candidate. If they were Black men, they were accused of being against a Black woman candidate, either out of envy or on general principles. As so often happens in Black life in the United States, emotions, charges, and countercharges clouded the fundamental issues. Few public figures raised valuable questions concerning the New Yorker's qualifications, her real chances, and the overall usages that the white, male-oriented power bloc could make out of a Black woman apparently carrying the burden for a group seemingly lacking suitable Black male candidates. Mrs. Chisholm, of course, did not consider herself the Black redeemer, antimale, nor a candidate for the women's liberation establishment, but she certainly must have pleased certain of their members and many sly, white male manipulators, in addition to and perplexing some Black people when she swore that she had been "more oppressed as a woman than as a Black."

When Ron Dellums, a supporter of Mrs. Chisholm, agreed

that there were indeed "new niggers" in the land, an ex-Beatle excitedly took the cue and made a recording, classifying "women as the niggers of the world." Whether or not many of the leaders and so-called Black leaders—women and men—are dancing to the tune of the white supremacists or unconsciously serving as their foils is somewhat irrelevant. What is more important is that the visible formalized Black "leadership" is always vulnerable to continued exploitation and manipulation by the oppressors.

The present situation is not nearly as simple as it was in the past. During the days of de jure slavery, it was easy to tell the "good guys" from the "bad guys"—the good guys called themselves "abolitionists" and usually lived "up North"; the bad guys generally lived "down South" and were slave masters (though there were some "good ones"), vicious overseers, slave breakers, and slave catchers. Today, slavery has become institutionalized and worldwide. Whereas, once control and exploitation of Blacks were handled by individual slave masters, social and governmental forces now assume the operation. All whites benefit whether they want to or not, and with a minimum of individual bigoted effort on their parts.

In the old days, a bad white was easy to spot; one could identify him by his geography, clothes, language, and deeds; but today, things have become infinitely more complex. In spite of the fact that many whites dress, talk, sing, and generally simulate different life-styles from their time-worn conventions, there is one area that they have not appreciably disturbed—the establishment of exploitative white supremacy. This is not to state that all whites are "bad," or that all Blacks are good, but that America (like her Western European parent) is a racist, capitalistic institution, and as such, all Blacks occupy an exploited class, or more precisely, caste, and all whites are materially benefited by Black oppression. A definite advantage to their position is that Black men occupy a niche a notch or two beneath Black women.

Many people in the country also apparently make distinctions as to how they view Black women and Black men who are accused of criminal activities. Two important people who have been involved in Black liberation efforts serve as clear examples.

When Angela Davis, a fighter for freedom, faced the ordeal of a court trial, she received massive interracial support that was both deserved and effective. H. Rap Brown, a former spokesman for many Black people and an advocate of Black Power, is incarcerated, virtually ignored by radical groups, both Black and white. To argue that Angela was a member of a well-organized group while Rap operated virtually unattached would be to miss the meaning of the overall situation and further point out the amorphous and dependent character of a significant element in the Black community.

Surely, few Blacks would ignore the implications and their responsibility by simply stating that Angela was obviously innocent, while Rap's case wasn't as clear. Would their position also explain the lack of active interest in the plights of numerous Black men now rotting in prisons? Angela Davis, B. B. King, James Baldwin, etc., and other less known Black people are working with prisoners and attempting to bring their predicaments to public attention. The list and programs are impressive but not overcrowded. More concern must be shown among the people and their leaders if the Browns, Ruchell McGees, George Jacksons, and the many others are not to be continuously brutalized and slaughtered.

It is extremely tragic in this era, when the degeneration of the West causes the forces of oppression to both escalate and sophisticate their exploitation and control over Africans throughout the world, that many Black so-called leaders in America, either from opportunism or romanticism, are seemingly sinking deeper into irrelevancy and impotency. The social straits and shortsightedness that too many Black leaders work under is but an open invitation to racial, or at least cultural, suicide in the face of America's very concrete anti-Black philosophies and practices.

Ironically, another group of verbose Blacks have arisen and made careers for themselves out of ignorantly and demagogically screaming half-truths and borrowed white lies. By playing on the neurotic fears, resentments, and insecurities of many of the oppressed, they have been able to peddle their wares, and further confuse the people. Black imprisonment and slavery are further secured as the people are feminized and emotionalized in preparation for their public pimping. Seemingly, few people advocate strength and autonomy in Black males, or circumspection and dignity in Black females.

Black people are offered emotional blind alleys, psychic drains and myriad frustrations. Admittedly, it is far easier for many Black people to continue pursuing opiates (in "partying," "church-shucking," and in drugs such as cocaine and heroin), displacement, and illusions than it would be to actually discover and deal with the real root causes of their plight. Those who try are often attacked and slandered by myopic opportunists. Malcolm X was virtually ignored or deprecated by many influential Black leaders and opinion-makers until after he died. Now even they, along with some white conveyors of pop trash are getting into the act. Today, the meaning of Malcolm's person and words have been largely avoided. A certain segment of the crowd actually twist his legacy into a selfish strategy of stealing with impunity; "by any means necessary" is a phrase which has been popularized and misunderstood. Instead of Blacks using that statement to pursue freedom, too often, many opportunists utilize it as a justification to "rip off" (im)material goods.

It seems obvious that racist white control over the thoughts and lives of Black people and Black unity are incompatible. A critical and autonomous reading of the actual problems facing Black people, however, can lead to real solutions. The opportunists and the dangerously naive must be educated or removed from the ranks of Black leadership. If realism does not prevail in the vital area of the Black struggle, Blacks will not lose on the "battlefield"; rather, they will not survive "boot camp":

> It has reached the critical stage that marriages, played by the rules of this sick society, find married couples have nothing in common but their names. These marriages are highly competitive. In order to survive together, they must first compete with the overwhelming odds in favor of event of separation or divorce. Secondly, they must

> stage strong competition with the oppressive system under
> which they live. . . . While in the process of battling for
> survival, they are both on the brink of self destruction.[4]

The genocide of Black people, especially in America, appears to be a distinct possibility. Disunity and distrust among Blacks are growing at alarming rates—the dissension between Black men and Black women is only a reflection and a reinforcement of total Black disunity; the difference in sex compounds the problem. It is time for all Black people to realize that in order for a slave society to continue operating it must have the cooperation of the slave, as well as the slave master.

An Ashanti proverb states, "The ruin of a nation begins in the home of its people." Blacks who are interested in not only survival but liberation would do well to turn to their ravished family structure and discover and attempt to uproot the slave values therein. For too long, Black leaders have operated on white-conditioned assumptions and ignored their abused family construction, and the most assaulted women and men within them who are inadvertent carriers of the sickness of, and logic for, slavery. This condition of Black complicity in their own slavery cannot be solved by rejecting even the most irascible Black women or the most irresponsible Black men, nor can it be changed by further misunderstanding the function and possibilities of the Black family and by expediently romanticizing the Black woman and condemning the Black man.

To be sure, the woman should be loved, supported, and challenged, but above all, understood. The man should be loved, supported, and challenged, and yes, understood. The Black woman's psyche (as all Black people's) has undergone a special form of cruel siege for over 300 years. No matter what Black entertainers say about how "beautiful," "foxy," and "queenly," etc., she is, the Black woman is affected as much as they are by the destructive influence of white control and ruthless materialism. She has been battered without and within by America's jack-in-the-box culture.

Many are pushed to frustration, bitterness, and self-deprecation. Many feel trapped in the "monster factories" (Paul Cook's term) in white society. Such factories create "niggers," Blacks who are programmed for self-destruction, who are under the exploitative and oppressive domination of Dr. Frankensteins. This domination causes an insecure female to disrespect and dislike her male counterpart, the man whom she supposedly loves. As she gets older and has more responsibilities to assume (usually children), her need for greater security within the capricious power of the society grows. Her toleration and patience diminish. She then begins to make more demands on her mate as one would do on an automobile stranded on a railroad track—the man, in time, actually becomes for her a machine, a thing. His value is determined by his practical effectiveness, his ability to make societal maneuvers (which almost always violate human integrity), not by his love, humanity, ideas and ideals, or aspirations and related abstractions. The train is approaching and she must leave the tracks, but she cannot leave her machine for it is the only one she has, and there are always other trains and other tracks. Thus, inadvertently, such a woman serves as an adjunct of the slave system—she is used to further limit the man's freedom, or to tighten his slavery.

The politically impotent and harried Black male sees the danger posed by the woman whom he loves. He desires her but he cannot cope with her intense insecurity, resentment, or her possessiveness. He has hated the prohibitions placed on him by white society; he cannot easily accept the restrictions proffered to him by a Black woman. Since the power to have and exercise responsibility is generally denied him, he seeks satisfaction with a minimum amount of personal commitment. In his desire to "be a man," to attain some freedom, some meaning, he often turns to the possibility easily accessible to him—sex. From childhood, Black males learn that there are doors that they must not open, lines that they must not cross. Some open or attempt to open, some cross, but all pay the price for their insolence. If they survive, they often join their less bold, more practical Brothers in the one area that they can enter.

Some Black men approach and value sexual conquests as many white males worship material acquisitions and becoming a respectable bank president or a successful bank embezzler. In the main, Brothers don't mean any harm—most have mothers whom they revere—but it just so happens that women have the means between their legs to give them instant transcendence and importance. The pity, of course, is that the feeling (with or without love) must be repeated over, over, and over again—the person of the woman might be incidental, the thighs are the things.

Black males do not view sex as many moralistic whites see it; sex is not an act that is nasty but necessary, nor is it a newly discovered reversible Puritan mechanical toy. It is the intense, pleasurable expression of a soulful man. For far too many Black men, however, especially poor ones, sexual intercourse is a substitute for the beginning and end of existence, and the space in between. Centuries of hell can be cooled by some leg. While the war is raging, they are scoring. To be sure, not all Black men succumb to the sex-only syndrome, as not all Black women turn into machine-moulding mamas—many of them understand the anti-Black character of the society and successfully combat it—but all Black people are assailed by the monstrosity and its effects.

Cut off from many areas of self-expression that are permitted to white males, some Black males seek to become the best at what is allowed them. For some, three very attractive choices are: athletics, entertainment, and pimping—not necessarily in that order. Needless to say, none of these occupations threaten the status quo. In the field of sports, the Brother can show his physical prowess and general superiority over the white man and make some money in the process; through entertaining, he can not only make "good" money, but satisfy his hungry ego, exhibit his talents, and easily qualify as an instant Black leader and expert on Black affairs.

The pimp is in a class all by himself, though the "cool pusher man" who makes more bread than he does is beginning to move in on the celebrated hustler's territory. The pimp does not have to adhere to dumb white boy's rules in a chump job—he owns some nice threads, boss wheels, and some foxy ladies. Upon reaching puberty, many young Bloods begin to sense the rules of the games, and though they realize that they cannot immediately get the most expensive clothes or a hog, they can and do buy a pair of "pimp socks" and start looking for the women.

The game begins—the boy wants to be hip and cool; he needs willing girls to be successful. The girls, many of whom have not had economically solid fathers, desire young men who can act as security symbols and, if a push comes to a shove, maybe love. The male learn how to "talk that talk," while the good-looking females begin to rate the fellows by their material possessions and by the hipness of their rap. Were it not for the demoralizing roles that they are forced to play, they might discover that they both are victims, but as it is, the game rules and their respective masks prevent them from knowing each other or themselves. Little honesty can transpire between the two people who have been forced to learn that the only way one survives is by doing "unto others before they do unto you."

The girl who has been fortunate enough to have received adequate protection from the worst aspects of the white society, and even some parental (father, as well as mother) love is a likely candidate for the ghettoized Black male's abuse. He feels forced to vent his pent-up rage and violence on her. The boy whose family provided a healthy background for him will be rejected as a square or exploited as a mark by the ghettoized hip girls. In the first case, the girl has to function as an accommodating, simple-minded thing to keep her man (individuals who live on instinct have little appreciation for thinking people; the shock is almost too much for fragile, fragmented egos), while in the second, the young man must learn to mistreat his woman in order to gain her respect. Masculine power, even if it is brutally applied, has great appeal to many oppressed masochistic females. Too often kindness, compassion, and gentleness are seen as definite signs of weakness.

From close observation, one might gather that rarely does a flexible, guileless Black woman and a flexible, guileless Black man ever get together. It seems that the serious young Black woman invariably is attracted to the nickle-slick Black man, and the serious young Black man idealizes the play-girl Black woman. One possible explanation, in the case of the serious naive woman, is that she has a predilection towards the flashier, jivier Brothers; thus, she brings about her own mistreatment and downfall. The serious inexperienced Brother, in his desire to "catch a 'beautiful' Sister," occasionally makes the mistake of confusing the beauty of the form with that of content; thus, he freely participates in his demise.

Too often, a once serious and trusting girl becomes a hurt, embittered woman. That pain, along with the regular mistreatment that she receives as a Black person in an anti-Black society, causes the injured woman to distrust and resent all Black men on general principles. She may renounce Black men and turn to white males or else seek solace and understanding from people of her own sex; if the aggrieved Sister remains with Black men and actually chooses one as her mate, she exacts a hard price for her sacrifice. She greatly assists white society in shaping him into a dull, obedient shell of a man.

The Black man who has been used and hurt by Black women will often seek other alternatives, the most noteworthy today being white women. Thus, many Black women will cry that they have been wronged by Black men, while many Black men will level the same charge against Black women. A greater truth, but one extremely difficult to deal with, is that they both have been wronged by the divisive thrust of the white racist society. Of course, there are some strong, understanding Black women and men who, through their love, form healthy and spiritually profound relationships; but even they must be aware of and ward off the societal-produced forces of distrust and divisiveness.

Yet, soft lies are easier to accept than hard truths. Black women and Black men rarely examine and analyze their rapidly eroding relationships in open forums. Too often when they have met to discuss their problems, the occasions have been marred by acrimony, intimidation, and general dissimulative posturing. Many people who baptize themselves in bogus nationalism do nothing to help the effort. In their inflexible insistence on summing up the world strictly in black and white terms, they attempt to force others to adopt their perspective, a perspective that rules out the actual nuances and complexities of life.

Though it is becoming increasingly apparent for all who care to see, few individuals have the courage to state an obvious fact: present-day unions between Black males and females are becoming so hazardous that a growing number of Brothers and Sisters would rather confront racist opposition from without, in a union with a non-Black person, than to face racist-related turmoil from within with an unconscious, victimized Black partner. On a purely personal level, without the vantage point of history, economics, and politics, one can understand why many Black people are declaring their "independence" from each other. Shortsighted independence for Black people, however, only serves to reinforce their dependency upon their oppressors.

The Black victims must not allow the self-hypnotic rhetoric of their leader-celebrities to blind them to the true nature of their oppression or to shield them from actual solutions to it. Black women are exploited as "niggers" as well as Black men—both will be treated as nothing else as long as they remain under the vicious control of the white supremacist, greed-ridden Western societies. Eventual freedom and complete humanization are possible but, in the main, still in the future. Now, Black degradation and slavery are a de facto reality. Blacks must admit, understand, and realistically deal with their oppression. "Blackenizing" romantic, opportunistic, reactionary cover-ups and approaches to real problems is no adequate substitute for accurate analyses and autonomous communal strategy.

Most assuredly, both sexes are in the same boat; if they do not pilot it together, they will drown separately. Instead of the two accusing each other of being wrong, they must realize that they have been and are being wronged. Power may come from guns, conformity may be forced, but spiritual unity can only emanate from freed minds. No approach, no matter how sensational, emotional, or commercially profitable it is will be effective, unless it takes into serious consideration the nature and immensity of the pathology surrounding Black people. It must comprehend the disastrous, disorienting effects that present-day Euro-American society has on the Black family and its members.

By the time that Black boys and girls discover that there is a societal-produced psychological barrier between them, it is almost too late to successfully combat it. Their tragedy is quadrupled when they both lack self-esteem. The emphasis on individual efforts, declarations of personal guilt and acrimony, and laudatory poetry will not by themselves suffice. The Black family and each member in it is under both political and psychological oppression, engineered by an organized predacious power. (Though human decency and the nation's own history demand that full reparation be made to Black people, I am convinced that America cannot beg, borrow, nor steal enough money to pay for the havoc she has wreaked on the Black family.) Black individual concerns and efforts must be subsumed under and directed by unified and community-oriented action.

If Black youths are to be saved from permanent psychic damage, it is absolutely imperative that they be provided with a safe, loving atmosphere, wherein spiritual and cultural support and healthy human alternatives can be preserved and presented to them. Out of their own weakness and confusion, far too many contemporary Black parents have allowed their children to be raised by alien and hostile groups and organizations. Television and motion pictures, two giant industries that are replete with racism, materialism, and pop nihilistic attitudes, are especially detrimental to Black life-styles and values; yet, Black young people tend to be their most enthusiastic and consistent fans. Even when they have chance encounters with Black individuals and groups who work for their welfare, these pitifully brainwashed people judge autonomous Blacks from the frame of references of their white exploiters and masters. Black families must be restored and strengthened, for if Black parents are not saved, there can be little hope for their children. Given their historical positions of influence in the family, the Black woman must exercise even more enlightened moral responsibility.

Indeed, if an immediate and gigantic effort is not made to

reconstruct the present terms under which Black lives are lived, and if the children are not saved all our pronouncements are simple prelude—or postlude—to the destruction of Black people in the United States of America and throughout the West.

NOTES

1. C. Eric Lincoln, "The Black Muslims," in *Justice Denied,* eds. William N. Chace and Peter Collier (New York: Harcourt, Brace and World, Inc.), p. 475.
2. Jamillah Muhammed, "Muhammed Speaks," in *Broken Images* (April, 1972), p. 18.
3. History is full of numerous, often aborted, attempts at liberation, by earlier unnamed slaves; by Toussaint the Savior, Gabriel, Denmark Vesey, Nat Turner, etc.; by Medgar Evers, George Jackson, and the Attica inmates. The list is inexhaustible.
4. Jamillah Muhammed, "Muhammad Speaks," in *Broken Images* (May 19, 1972), p. 18.